Perceval Clark

Index to Trevelyan's Life and Letters of Lord Macaulay

Perceval Clark

Index to Trevelyan's Life and Letters of Lord Macaulay

ISBN/EAN: 9783337012403

Printed in Europe, USA, Canada, Australia, Japan

Cover: Foto ©ninafisch / pixelio.de

More available books at **www.hansebooks.com**

INDEX TO LIFE OF MACAULAY.

INDEX SOCIETY.
PUBLICATIONS, 1879.
VI.

INDEX

TO

TREVELYAN'S LIFE AND LETTERS

OF

LORD MACAULAY.

(CABINET EDITION, 1878.)

BY

PERCEVAL CLARK.

LONDON:
PUBLISHED FOR THE INDEX SOCIETY
BY LONGMANS, GREEN & Co., 39, PATERNOSTER ROW.
MDCCCLXXXI.

PREFACE.

It will not be thought necessary to urge the claims of Biography generally to be represented in the Index Society, seeing that if it cannot appeal to any special class of searchers, it is only because there is no province of literature which does not fall under its sway, no toilers in the field of Letters who have not something to do with the study of the lives of others. Nor will Index-lovers, who are fond of Macaulay's writings, look for any reason for the appearance of this Index beyond the bare fact that Mr. Trevelyan sent his book into the world without its 'bag and baggage.' But if it were necessary to reason the need of the thing, without stopping to consider whether this Life of Macaulay is to be ranked among great English biographies or no, it might be held sufficient to run the eye over nearly any page of this Index, and note the number of men famous above their kind in the most varied walks of life. In one page will be found specified entries under the names of Bulwer Lytton, Bunyan, Buonaparte, and Burke; in another Lord Carlisle and Thomas Carlyle face us cheek by jowl; in a third, Dickens and Disraeli, or Gibbon and Gladstone, or Southey, de Staël and Stanley, show the rich and varied nature of the deposit, which this shaft has been sunk to reach. An American thought that the sublimest of all spectacles would be Macaulay standing by Wordsworth's grave; from another point of view it is equally interesting to hear what Macaulay has to say about Eugene Sue, Swift, Talleyrand, Tennyson, Kate Terry, Thackeray, Thiers and Thirlwall—names that lie as close neighbours on the opening of two pages. Or, taking the list of subjects discussed by him for reviewing, to picture another volume of "Critical and Historical Essays" containing articles on Jane Austen, Richardson's Novels, Edmund Burke, Bishop Burnet, Napoleon, Dickens's *American Notes*, Hannah More, Lord Shaftesbury, and Voltaire—a collection which might well be noted in some future "Curiosities of Literature," as one of the events which have not happened in the world of Letters. Or to glean how he ranked the great poets and historians of all time, what he held to be the best and worst things in Greek and Latin, to learn what were his favourites of the plays of Shakespeare, Molière and Schiller, of Cities, Bishops and Statesmen; to note his habits of reading, and love of poring over lists and calendars; to be able to picture his appearance and dress and manner; to gather up his thoughts and remarks, whether on religion and politics, or on olive-trees and the ex-lions of London fashion; to share with him for a moment the charms of his college life in London, or to wander forth from his library into the 'xystus,' or on to the clean-shaven lawn of Holly Lodge, while he is pouring forth unwieldy French with De Tocqueville, discussing with Ticknor the merits of Burke as a possible historian, or deluging his listeners like a waterspout with the marvels of his memory.

For it is not the "all-knowingness" of Macaulay—to quote

PREFACE. vii

Sir James Stephen's expression—that has riveted the attention of those who have read the memoir of his life, so much as the human sympathy for which those who knew him only through his writings had been somehow or other loth to give him credit. Diligent students of the *Essays* and the *History* were pleasantly surprised to find that the author had a heart after all, and a heart which was nothing if not emotionable, that he could love little children and admire beautiful women,[1] enjoy life as an Epicurean, and practise virtue as a Stoic; that while the Athenæum Club held its breath at the current rumour that he was reading for pleasure the two hundred and seventy-nine critical reviews of Photius, he had the greatest zest for romantic trash, could revel among the fainting-fits of "Santo Sebastiano," discuss with relish every marble-covered volume that was issued, and repeat by the yard the sorriest of doggrel rhyme. It is this "seemingly boundless knowledge of life," as Colonel Meadows Taylor wrote of him in India, his interest in all things and all men, that lend a value to any allusions to the scenes and characters of the drama in which Macaulay played so important a part, whence it cannot but be that the historian of the annals or literature of England for an important part of the nineteenth century must turn to Macaulay's Life, as being that of one who was honoured in his generation and a glory of his time.

The single heading MACAULAY of course takes up a large space of this Index, and will be found, together with a few

[1] Ticknor, the historian of Spanish literature, writes in 1857: "Then I drove out to Macaulay's, who seemed uncommonly glad to see me, and talked after his fashion for half an hour with great richness and knowledge, chiefly on female beauty, which, by the most curious citations from Lady M. Wortley Montagu's letters, from Sir C. Grandison, Congreve's plays, and such out-of-the-way places, he proved had greatly increased in England since the disappearance of small-pox."

other headings, of which a list is given at page 45, to contain everything directly touching him. The list of his published writings (beginning, it will interest the Members of the Index Society to note, with an INDEX) refers of course only to writings mentioned by his Biographer, and lays no claim to be considered an exhaustive bibliography of his works. The books Macaulay read that were "mostly trash," have their places in the body of the Index, while those that stood by him in all vicissitudes as comforters, nurses, and companions, have half a page to themselves under one of the sections of MACAULAY. The particulars of his life and work in India are given under INDIA; localities in London under LONDON; various newspapers under NEWSPAPERS, and certain French and Italian towns visited by Macaulay under their countries respectively. Peers are arranged under their titles, save when they are mostly known in the *Life* by their family names, as Charles Grant, Stanley, Sir Charles Wood, and others; Bishops and Deans under their family names. Pains have been taken to prefix the Christian name or its initial to such surnames as are without it, and to give to hereditary titles their right numerical designation.

The cabinet edition of 1878 has been used for two reasons: it contains somewhat more matter than the first edition does; and from its size is one of those books that, as Dr. Johnson said, "form the mass of general and easy reading."

It is only right to state that this Index is published with Mr. Trevelyan's sanction and goodwill.

PERCEVAL CLARK.

BEDFORD PARK, CHISWICK.

INDEX

TO

TREVELYAN'S LIFE OF MACAULAY.

ABERCROMBIE "on the Intellectual Powers," a suggested prize-book for an Indian college, i. 418.
ABERCROMBY, Right Hon. J., Speaker, raised to the peerage, ii. 64.
ABERDEEN, 4th Earl of, Prime Minister, his estimate of *Macbeth*, ii. 203; in the board-room of the British Museum, ii. 205; at Windsor Castle, ii. 296; his stories of the Scotch Judges, ii. 296; his taciturnity corrected, ii. 310; appointed Prime Minister, ii. 340; his resignation, ii. 390*n*.; as an orator, ii. 57.
Academy, Royal, ii. 113; Macaulay elected Professor of Ancient Literature, ii. 307*n*.; dinner at, in 1852, ii. 307.
ACHILLES TATIUS, i. 465, 466*n*.
ADAM, William, his duel with Fox, i. 240.
ADAM, Admiral, son of preceding, i. 240.
ADDINGTON, Right Hon. H. (Lord Sidmouth), Macaulay's estimate of, ii. 275 *sq.*
ADDISON, Joseph, failed in Parliament, i. 179; a favourite of Macaulay's, i. 427 *sq.*; a model of pure writing, ii. 108 *sq.*; his *Spectators*, ii. 138*n*.; *alluded to*, i. 134, 428; ii. 9, 113, 395, 455, 490. See *Aikin*.
ADEANE, H., M.P. for Cambridgeshire, at Cambridge during an election, i. 76.
ADELAIDE, Queen, at the coronation of William IV., i. 250.
ADOLPHUS, J. L., his criticism of the *Lays of Rome*, ii. 120 *sq.*, 257; writes kindly to Macaulay about the *History*, ii. 394.
Advertisement, a rhyming, ii. 366.
ÆLIAN, ii. 472.
ÆSCHINES, statue of, in the Vatican, ii. 33; ii. 433.

1

ÆSCHYLUS, one of the six first-rate Athenian writers, ii. 433; i, 437, 452, 481 *sq.*; ii. 304 *sq.*; compared with Milton, ii. 432 *sq.*; *quoted*, i. 444, 481.

AGUESSEAU, H. F. D', Chancellor of France, ii. 258.

AIKIN, Lucy, her Life of Addison, ii. 128; annoyed by Macaulay's article on, ii. 129, 259 *sq.*; her book full of blunders, ii. 130, 131*n.*, 263.

AIRY, George B. (afterwards Sir George), entertains Macaulay and his sisters at Cambridge, i. 183.

AKENSIDE, Mark, estimate of his poetical powers, i. 341; Johnson's opinion of, i. 341.

ALBANY, Countess of, ii. 23.

ALBANY, The. See *London.*

ALBEMARLE, 4th Earl of, at Holland House, i. 213.

ALBERT, Prince, offers Macaulay the Cambridge Professorship of Modern History, ii. 265; his remark on University Professorships of Medicine, ii. 295; attacks made on him in 1854 in connection with Russian negociations, ii. 376 *sq.*

ALCIBIADES, i. 453*n.*

Aldine Classics; no Greek authors in public library of Venice, ii. 417; at Althorp, ii. 433; Panizzi's estimate of, ii. 450.

Aldingham, living of, given to Rev. J. Macaulay, ii. 264.

ALEXANDER I., Emperor of Russia, i. 91.

ALEXANDER THE GREAT, his feeling towards the orators, ii. 198; his glory compared with that of Homer, ii. 215; his conquests spread the knowledge of Greek in Asia, ii. 472.

Alexandria, Dr. Parr on pronunciation of its name, ii. 429.

Alexandrian Library, destruction of, i. 416.

ALFIERI, his tomb at Florence, ii. 23.

ALLEN, John, friend of Lord Holland, at Holland House, i. 213 *sq.*, 280, 282; how treated by Lady Holland, i. 241, 264, 273 *sq.*, 347, 360.

ALLEN, William, the Quaker, ii. 51.

Almanach des Gourmands, Macaulay fond of quoting, i. 296; ii. 410–412, 411*n.*, 412*n.*

ALTHORP, Lord (3rd Earl Spencer), his habits and character, i. 246–248, 265; ii. 275; his opinion of Macaulay's eloquence and official ability, i. 234, 316 *sq.*, 320; his share in the Sheil affair, i. 364–366; *alluded to,* i. 245*n.*, 306; ii. 38.

Althorp, Lord Spencer's seat, i. 213; ii. 274, 433.

ALVANLEY, Lord, i. 213, 328.

America, American; Macaulay's correspondents, i. 266, 268; ii. 202 *sq.*, 299, 393; consul at Rome, ii. 35; clergyman at Florence,

America (*continued*):—
ii. 36*n*.; a wish about Macaulay and Wordsworth's tomb, ii.
481; statesmen's view of British Government appointments, ii.
384; Repudiation paper, ii. 197; *North American Review* quoted,
ii. 384*n*.; Macaulay described in a New York paper, ii. 210;
publication of *Edinburgh Review* articles in, ii. 112, 125 and
note; and of the *History*, ii. 240, 397; its best published work,
ii. 329; a publisher's request made to Macaulay, ii. 393.
AMESBURY, Lord, i. 264.
AMMIANUS MARCELLINUS, i. 466.
AMPELIUS, i. 456, 467.
ANDERSEN, Hans, allusion to a fairy tale of, ii. 324.
ANDERSON, G. W., Member of Indian Jurisprudence Commission, in 1835, i. 421.
ANECDOTES, STORIES, etc. Lord Braxfield at whist, ii. 296; the fatted calf and mock turtle, ii. 330; the cat at a Cambridge election, i. 76; Chantrey and his table, i. 231; King Christian of Denmark, i. 278; Christians of Tanjore and the Bible, i. 384; Lord Clive and the lac of rupees, ii. 350 *sq.*, 351*n*.; the quoting Doctor, i. 443*n*.; the Duchess and her sailor son, i. 324 *sq.*; the gamecocks, i. 23; Rowland Hill, ii. 199; visit of a Quaker to his chapel, i. 21; Lord Holt and the Holy Ghost, ii. 203*n*.; Bishop Horsley and "the mass of the people," i. 162; Lord Londonderry's pious resignation, ii. 120; Macaulay and the barber, i. 123; —— and the hearse, ii. 300; —— on his riding powers, i. 123; Sir W. Maule on schools, i. 39; the young man in the Oxford coach, i. 284; Dr. Parr and Alexandria, ii. 429; a dream about *Pepys's Diary*, ii. 428; Bobus Smith on mosquitoes, i. 358; Sir John Sinclair's letter to Pitt, ii. 201; two distinctions mentioned in his works, ii. 201; Talleyrand, remarks by, i. 237 *sq.*; a translation from Theophrastus made at an examination, i. 453; Wellington and the Catholic Relief Bill, i. 163*n*.; —— and the Staff officer, ii. 281.
ANGLESEA, Marquis of, his fête in 1820, i. 106.
Anglo-Catholics. See *Puseyitism*.
ANNE, Queen, struggles between Whigs and Tories at close of her reign, i. 239; Macaulay's knowledge of the literature of the time of, ii. 455.
ANSON's "Voyage," i. 418.
Anti-Corn Law League, its leaders defeated at General Election of 1857, ii. 440. See *Corn Laws*.
Anti-Slavery question, i. 312-326.

APOLLONIUS RHODIUS, i. 452.
APPLEYARD, ——, Macaulay's cicerone at Althorp, ii. 274.
Applicants, Macaulay's; P——, i. 338; a place-hunter in India, i. 431n.; Leigh Hunt, ii. 125; the lady asking for three livings and a bishopric, ii. 181; demand of a loan of £50, ii. 290; the philologist, ii. 424n.; *various*, ii. 422–424.
APTHORPE, Dr. East, a hostile critic of Gibbon, ii. 289n.
AQUINAS, THOMAS, i. 90.
Arabian Nights, The, references to, i. 88, 418, ii. 251n., 276, 298.
Arabic literature in India. See *India*.
ARBUTHNOT, Dr. John, his *John Bull*, ii. 393 and note; Macaulay's intimate knowledge of his pasquinades, ii. 455.
ARBUTHNOT, Right Hon. Charles, confidential friend of Duke of Wellington, ii. 253.
ARGYLL, Duchess of, wife of 8th Duke, recommends Holly Lodge to Macaulay, ii. 403.
ARGYLL, 8th Duke of, neighbour and friend of Macaulay, ii. 406, 481, 489.
ARIOSTO, a favourite of Macaulay's, i. 361, 379, 478; ii. 109; ranked by him before Virgil, ii. 202; *Thalaba* compared by Southey to *Orlando*, ii. 469.
"Aristarchus of Edinburgh," i. 168.
ARISTOPHANES, one of Macaulay's six first-rate Athenians, ii. 433; a favourite with him, i. 452 *sq.*, 455, 469; ii. 261, 304, 431, 459.
ARISTOTLE, his *Politics*, i. 448, 452; i. 473.
ARNOLD, Rev. F., his *Public Life of Macaulay* quoted, ii. 320n., 424.
ARRIAN, his *Expedition of Alexander*, i. 465.
ASHBURTON, 2nd Lord, Macaulay and Carlyle meet at house of, i. 8, ii. 199n.; on Indian Civil Service Committee, in 1854, ii. 380n.
Asia, the ship which conveyed Macaulay to India, i. 358; ii. 287.
Aspenden Hall, Mr. Preston's school, i. 51–60; ii. 401.
ATHANASIUS, read by Macaulay in India, i. 473.
ATHENÆUS, i. 449, 452, 470.
Athenian writers, the six first-rate, ii, 433.
Athens, Temple of the Winds at, ii. 110.
Athos, Mount, and Alexander of Macedon, i. 91.
ATTERBURY, Bishop, Macaulay's intimate knowledge of his writings, ii. 455.
ATTILA, Fred. Will. III. of Prussia likened to, ii. 32.
AUBIGNÉ, D'. See *Merle d'Aubigné*.
AUBIN, ——, British Chargé-d'Affaires at Florence in 1838, ii. 27.

AUCKLAND, 2nd Lord, Governor-General of India, sworn in at Calcutta,
i. 470; the Whigs try to save him from recrimination in 1843,
ii. 139; at Lord J. Russell's during the formation of a Cabinet,
ii. 171.
AUCKLAND, 3rd Lord, Bishop of Sodor and Man, his admiration for
Macaulay's *History*, ii. 237; his saying about the wisdom of
agreeing with Macaulay at once, ii. 237.
Augustan History, The, i. 458, 466; ii. 268; a book well known by
Macaulay, ii. 431.
AUGUSTINE, St., his *Confessions*, i. 474; ii. 302.
AULUS GELLIUS, a favourite of Macaulay's, i. 458; a marginal note in,
i. 238*n*.
AURELIUS VICTOR, i. 456.
AUSTEN, Jane, the third woman of her age, i. 246; Macaulay's
admiration of her novels, ii. 298, 387, 477; his project of writing
an article on, i. 363; he wishes to put up a monument to her,
ii. 477; a correction of his in *Persuasion*, ii. 477 and note;
characters in her novels, i. 135, 304 and note, 322 and note, 324
and note, 355 and note; ii. 210, 410.
AUSTIN, Charles, college contemporary of Macaulay, i. 78–80; ii. 438;
a day's conversation between him and Macaulay at Bowood, i. 80;
at Macaulay's breakfasts, ii. 198, 256; confirms a statement of
Macaulay about Procopius, ii. 243; his death, i. 78*n*.
AYTOUN, Professor, at the Edinburgh election of 1847, ii. 190.

" BABBLE-TONGUE MACAULAY, MR.," appellation of *The Times* for
Macaulay in 1839, ii. 70.
BABINGTON, ——, a nephew of Z. Macaulay, i. 37, 129, 280.
BABINGTON, George, a cousin of Macaulay, i. 125, 333, 358.
BABINGTON, Thomas, of Rothley Temple, married Jean Macaulay, i. 8;
his industry on the Slave-trade question, i. 64, 73; Macaulay
asked to write an epitaph for, ii. 230*n*.; *alluded to*, i. 12, 152,
184; ii. 3, 53.
BACON (Francis), Viscount St. Albans, his *De Augmentis*, i. 379; ii.
138*n*.; *Essays*, i. 418, 462; *Novum Organum*, ii. 138*n*.; mention
of, i. 99; ii. 193, 439; *quoted*, ii. 10, 407. See *Macaulay—
Writings*.
BAGEHOT, Walter, his praise of Macaulay's account of the origin of
the Bank of England, ii. 227.
BAILLIE, Joanna, a character in one of her plays, i. 481.
Ballads, Macaulay's collection of, ii. 96 and note; old English, ii. 121;
No Popery ——, ii. 200*n*.

BANCROFT, R., Archbishop of Canterbury, i. 206.
BANCROFT's *History of America*, ii. 299.
Bank of England, its origin well told by Macaulay, ii. 227.
Baptists at Sierra Leone, i. 23.
Barber, the Madras, famous for doggrel, i. 54n.; Macaulay's reply to one, i. 123.
BARHAM, Lord, report of death of, in 1832, i. 264.
BARING, Sir Francis, 1st Bart., i. 40.
BARING, Sir Francis, 3rd Bart., i. 235; ii. 171.
BARING, Sir Thomas, 2nd Bart., i. 239.
BARINGS, The, i. 210.
Barley Wood, Hannah More's residence, i. 34; ii. 401; Macaulay's visit in 1807, i. 34, 35 and note; ii. 303; visit in 1852, ii. 325-327, 329.
BARLOW, J., college contemporary of Macaulay, i. 99.
Barnaby's Journeys, ii. 291.
BARNES, Thomas, Editor of *The Times*, and Macaulay's squib on the Cambridge election, i. 233.
BARRON, Captain, i. 429.
BARROT, Camille, his speeches about England on the Eastern Question in 1840, ii. 83.
BARRY, Alexander [Baring?], M.P. in 1831, i. 208.
BARRY, J., historical painter, ii. 269.
BAVIUS, the malevolent critic of Virgil and Horace, ii. 393.
BEALES, Edmond, college contemporary of Macaulay, i. 117.
Beast of *Revelation*, Buonaparte and the House of Commons made out to be the, i. 377 *sq*.
BEATTIE, Dr., his *Life of Campbell*, ii. 251.
BEAUCHAMP, Countess. See *Stanhope*.
BEAUCLERK, Topham, Talleyrand's conversation likened by Macaulay to that of, i. 237.
BEAUMARCHAIS, P. A. C. de, French comic dramatist, his dealings with the Goëzmans, ii. 362, 363 and note.
BEDFORD, John, 4th Duke of, his character considered, ii. 100n.
BEHN, Afra, some of Defoe's writings on a moral level with those of, ii. 465; Mrs. Keith's opinion of her, ii. 465n.
BELPER, Lord. See *Strutt*.
BELSHAM, William, mentioned as a writer of bad history, ii. 322.
BENETT, John, M.P. for South Wilts in 1831, i. 239.
BENTHAM, Jeremy, assailed by Macaulay in *Edinburgh Review*, i. 140.
BENTINCK, Lady William, her welcome to the Macaulays in India, i. 370, 389.

BENTINCK, Lord William, Governor-General of India 1828-1835; at Ootacamund, i. 369 *sq.*; his welcome to Macaulay, i. 376; his description of Macaulay, i. 389; his kindness to C. Trevelyan, i. 392, and high opinion of him, i. 436; decides on the vexed question of Education in India, i. 411; his return home recorded by Macaulay, i. 470; Macaulay's estimate of, i. 376, 378, 392; ii. 79; statue of in Calcutta, i. 376; ii. 79 and note; description of, by Jacquemont, ii. 79.

BENTLEY, Joanna, daughter of the critic, Byrom's lines to, ii. 366*n*.

BENTLEY, Richard, Macaulay's estimate of his character and powers, ii. 243*n*., 244*n*.; comparison between his mind and Porson's, ii. 293; his pronunciation of Alexandria, ii. 429; his emendations in Milton, i. 446; in Ampelius, i. 467; the Phalaris controversy, i. 472; ii. 40*n*.; Macaulay's admiration of his scholarship, ii. 40*n*.; an emendation worthy of, ii. 477.

BERESFORD, Lord George, mentioned with reference to General Election of 1826, i. 146.

BERKELEY, Bishop, metaphysician, ii. 248.

BERRI, Duc de, ii. 144.

BERRY, Miss, a favourite of H. Walpole, i. 337, 346; figures in *Vivian Grey*, i. 346; her dislike to Macaulay's article on Walpole, i. 337, 340; her wish to collect Macaulay's *Edinburgh Review* articles, ii. 50; Macaulay at her house, i. 346; ii. 251; *alluded to*, i. 306, 363.

BETTY, H., "the young Roscius," an instance of a discarded favourite, ii. 252*n*.

Beverley, its M.P.s and bull-baiting, ii. 185.

Bible, quoted by Christians of Tanjore, i. 384; Macaulay's use of in learning languages, i. 461; Laponian New Testament, ii. 384; Luther's New Testament, i. 473; Gallio, i. 384; *Revelation*, i. 377; *Epistle to Romans*, ii. 337*n*.; St. John, i. 378; text of the Three Witnesses, ii. 294; parable of the Talents, i. 214; cities of the Levites, ii. 44.

Bible Society, its origin to be found in Clapham Sect, i. 69*n*.; a proposed branch of it in Wales, i. 105; at Cambridge, ii. 439; an Hibernian, i. 269.

Bibles, pictures in old, an early association of Macaulay's, ii. 417.

BIDEN, Captain, a Calcutta orator in connection with the *Black Act* of 1836, i. 406.

Biographia Britannica, i. 379.

BIRD, C. S., tutor of a Cambridge reading party in 1821, i. 104 *sq.*

Birmingham, Priestley riot in 1791 at, i. 162; political meeting in 1832 at, i. 259.

BLACK, Adam (of Edinburgh), Macaulay's letter to him on subject of giving a race-cup to his constituents, ii. 185 *sq.*; describes the Edinburgh defeat in 1847, ii. 190; his remark on the success of Macaulay's *History*, ii. 250; his speech advocating Macaulay's return to Parliament in 1852, ii. 313; writes to Craig on the subject, ii. 316; communicates to Macaulay his apprehensions on the same subject, ii. 317; is answered, ii. 318; sends news about it, ii. 319; presides at the Edinburgh meeting of Nov. 2, 1852, ii. 337; quoted in reference to Macaulay's contributions to Encyclopædia Britannica, ii. 456.

BLACKBURN, P., candidate for Edinburgh at the General Election of 1847, ii. 189–191.

BLACKMORE, R., poetaster, ii. 393.

Blackwood's Magazine, its criticism on the Sadler controversy, i. 128*n.*; its hostility to Macaulay on account of his *Edinburgh Review* articles, i. 141 *sq.*; a description of Macaulay quoted from, i. 244; its defence of Croker's *Boswell*, i. 255; its praise of the *Lays of Rome*, ii. 122 *sq.*

BLAIR, Hugh, *Life of*, ii. 292.

Blaise Castle, near Clifton, ii. 325.

BLEWITT, R. J., M.P. for Monmouth, mentioned in a poem by Praed, ii. 60.

BLOMFIELD, C. J., Bishop of London, preaches at coronation of William IV., i. 250; admires the style of Velleius Paterculus, i. 476; a member of *The Club* in 1839, ii. 53*n.*; there tells anecdotes about Rowland Hill, ii. 199; his thanksgiving at the closing ceremonial of Great Exhibition of 1851, ii. 210; entertains Macaulay at dinner, ii. 310; becomes warm on the subject of clairvoyance, ii. 311.

BLUNDELL, ——, a school-fellow of Macaulay, i. 41.

BOCCACCIO, Macaulay's boyish delight in, i. 59; the famous edition of the *Decameron* at Althorp, ii. 274; *alluded to*, i. 231; ii. 48.

BODDINGTON, Samuel, Macaulay dines with, i. 306, 357.

BOEHMEN, Jacob, *alluded to*, i. 21.

BOIARDO, Panizzi's reprint of, Macaulay discusses as a subject for an article, i. 390; he prefers him as a poet to Ovid, i. 478; reads him at Florence, ii. 22.

BOILEAU, an early favourite of Macaulay, i. 85; *quoted*, i. 149.

BOLINGBROKE, 1st Lord, Macaulay's early acquaintance with his writings, ii. 455; his "stupid infidelity," ii. 391; cited as an instance of early distinction indicating later success, ii. 352.

BONAPARTE. See *Buonaparte*.

BONNER, Bishop, i. 433.
Bookstalls. See *Macaulay—Miscellaneous Notes.*
BOSSUET, compared as a theologian with Fra Paolo, ii. 288.
BOSWELL, James, meets Macaulay's grandfather, i. 6 and *note*; Lawrence's sketch of him, i. 233; his signature in the Records of *The Club*, ii. 53*n*.; Macaulay gets his *Life of Johnson* as a prize, i. 419; Croker's edition of it, i. 233; *quotations* from the *Life* and the *Tour to the Hebrides* —— visit to Inverary Castle, i. 6*n*.; Langton and "unidea'd girls," i. 190*n*.; Johnson and the goats, ii. 216*n*.; Johnson and Hannah More, i. 233*n*.
BOTTA'S *History of the American War*, Macaulay's criticism on, ii. 47 *sq*.
BOWOOD, Lord Lansdowne's seat in Wilts, Sir W. Stirling Maxwell meets Macaulay there in 1852, i. 54*n*.; Austin and Macaulay at, i. 81; Macaulay stays there in 1830, i. 156 *sq*.; in 1833, i. 353; Macaulay and the "sociable cur" at, ii. 414.
BOWRING, Sir John, British Minister in China in 1857, ii. 434*n*.
BRAXFIELD, Lord, anecdote of, ii. 296.
BREWSTER, Sir David, and the clairvoyante, ii. 310.
BRIGHT, Dr., physician, ii. 295, 321 *sq*., 331.
BRIGHT, Right Hon. John, M.P., disapproves of the India Bill of 1853, ii. 347; in Parliament refers to the banquet given to Sir C. Napier in 1854, ii. 377; how alluded to by Palmerston in reply, ii. 377; defeated at the General Election of 1857, ii. 440.
Brighton, the Macaulays there in 1816, i. 61; in 1822, i. 86; hotel at, ii. 145; Macaulay's visits to his sisters at, ii. 259; he writes the *Encycl. Brit.* article on Bunyan there, ii. 259.
BRISCOE, J. J., M.P. for East Surrey in 1833, i. 301.
British Museum. See *London*.
BRODIE, Sir Benjamin, i. 218; ii. 295.
BROGLIE, Duc de, Councillor of State under Louis XVIII., corresponds with Z. Macaulay, i. 66; welcomes Macaulay in Paris in 1830, i. 169, 201; his *salon*, i. 171.
BROGLIE, Duc de, Leader of the Monarchists during Macmahon's Presidency, i. 171.
BROOK, Lord, killed at Lichfield in 1643, ii. 218.
BROOKE, Sir J., Rajah of Sarawak, meets Macaulay at dinner, ii. 310.
BROUGHAM, Lord Chancellor, his regard for Z. Macaulay, i. 66; ii. 12; introduces him to Jeffrey, i. 67; the advocate of Queen Caroline, i. 101; for long the main hope of the Anti-Slavery party, i. 101; goes the Northern Circuit, i. 148 *sq*.; ii. 324; his

BROUGHAM, Lord Chancellor (*continued*):—
popularity in 1830, i. 162; introduces Macaulay to La Fayette, i. 169; returned in 1830 M.P. for Yorkshire, i. 172; is the object of dread to a timid orator in Parliament, ii. 282*n*.; becomes Chancellor, i. 174; is defended in Parliament by Macaulay against Croker, i. 174; his jealousy on the subject of the Catholic Relief Bill, i. 192; wants Macaulay to review his speech on slavery in the *Edinburgh*, i. 201 *sq.*; at William IV.'s coronation, i. 250 *sq.*; meets Macaulay in 1839, ii. 51 *sq.*; objects to Macaulay's account of the first Lord Holland, ii. 97 *sq.*; doubts about the pronunciation of "Euripides," ii. 260; calumniously attacks Lord Rutherford in 1856, ii. 441*n*.; Macaulay's opinion of him—generally, i. 148 *sq.*, 191-194; ii. 441 and note; ii. 25; —of his mental and literary powers, i. 328, 393; ii. 11, 153; —of his eloquence, i. 175, ii. 47, 153; respecting his connection with the *Edin. Rev.* i. 191 *sq.*, 203 *sq.*; ii. 10 *sq.*; and his abuse of the Whigs, ii. 11, 139; his feeling towards Macaulay, i. 158, 171, 191, 203-205; ii. 12, 97, 260; his bearing towards others— Burdett, i. 192; Denman, i. 158; Lord Durham, ii. 24-26, 51; Jeffrey, i. 191 *sq.*; the Mills, i. 191 *sq.*; Napier, i. 171 *sq.*, 203; ii. 15; Lord Plunket, i. 192; Pollock, i. 149; ii. 324; the Whig party, ii. 11 *sq.*; *alluded to*, i. 98, 154, 240, 242, 273, 296; ii. 104, 111.

BROUGHAM, William, brother of the Chancellor, i. 279.
BROUGHTON, Lord. See *Hobhouse*.
BROWN, Robert, botanist, i. 283.
BRUCE, Lord Justice Knight, suggests the offer of a Lincoln's Inn Benchership to Macaulay, ii. 277*n*.
BRUCE, T. C., candidate for Edinburgh at the General Election of 1852, ii. 319.
BUCCLEUCH, 5th Duke of, ii. 46.
BUCKINGHAM, 2nd Duke of, ii. 165.
BUCKINGHAM, J. Silk, ii. 122, 258.
Buckingham Palace, Macaulay at, ii. 265, 279.
BUCKLE, H. T., his testimony to Macaulay's accuracy quoted, ii. 227 *sq.*; Macaulay's estimate of, ii. 470*n*.
BULLER, Charles, in the House of Commons, ii. 78; his death, ii. 249; Macaulay's mention of him in speech at Edinburgh, in 1852, ii. 249*n*.
BULLER, Sir J. Yarde, his motion of want of confidence in 1840, ii. 74; Macaulay's speech on, a failure, ii. 75*n*.

BULWER LYTTON, Edward Lytton, Lord Lytton; an early walk with Macaulay in 1831, i. 245; an admirer of Macaulay, i. 245; editor of *New Monthly Magazine*, i. 246; asks Macaulay to contribute to it, i. 246; gives up the editorship, i. 329, 331; his first Parliamentary success in 1833, i. 297; his dress, i. 329; his novel *Pelham*, ii. 41, 44n.; *My Novel*, ii. 43n.; *Alice*, ii. 43; Macaulay's estimate of, ii. 43 and note, 44n.; *Last Days of Pompeii*, ii. 45 sq.; his poem *St. Stephen's*, ii. 142n, 179; his remarks on Macaulay's speeches in Parliament, ii. 142n., 143n.; his scheme for a literary association, ii. 293; made D.C.L. of Oxford in 1856, ii. 399n.; alluded to, in Praed's squib, ii. 61.

BUNSEN, Chevalier, ii. 399n.

BUNYAN, John; *Pilgrim's Progress*, Macaulay could have reproduced it from recollection, i. 53; his review of it, i. 195; no copy of, in the Athenæum Club, i. 195; Pontine Marshes likened to certain scenes in, ii. 42; "Pliable," ii. 414; his *Grace Abounding*, ii. 302.

BUONAPARTE, Napoleon, Macaulay's boyish reflections on his exile to Elba, i. 50; his fall in 1815 a Tory triumph, i. 162; bust of, at Holland House, i. 219; made out to be the "Beast" of Revelation, i. 377; his Codes, i. 423; his victories depicted at Versailles, ii. 49; at Schönbrunn after Austerlitz, ii. 71; Capefigue's history of the Consulate and Empire of, ii. 80; his health proposed at a literary dinner by Campbell, ii. 251n.; *quoted*, i. 194, 460; remark made by an old soldier of, i. 170.

BURDETT, Sir Francis, his remark to Brougham, i. 192; alluded to, i. 244; ii. 332.

BURGESS, Bishop, his trash in answer to Porson's Letters to Travis, ii. 293.

BURKE, Edmund, Disraeli's allusion to, in *Young Duke*, i. 230n; Macaulay's admiration of, ii. 385; estimate of his oratory and political exertions, i. 179, 451; not a poet, ii. 124; Macaulay projects a review of his life and writings, ii, 155n.; mention of, in Essay on *Hastings*, i. 261; Macaulay's eloquence likened to his, i. 177, 317, and note; his writings, ii. 138n.; his pamphlets, ii. 113, 455; his saying about Henry IV. of France *quoted*, i. 91.

BURKE, Sir John, i. 270.

Burleigh, Elizabethan mansion of the Cecils, i. 434.

Burmese Emperor, the, i. 264.

BURNET, Bishop, a favourite author of Macaulay's, i. 61, 339; Macaulay's project of an article on his *Characters* edited by Jebb, i. 390; his *History of my own Times*, ii. 322.

BURNET, Thomas, author of *Telluris Theoria Sacra*, ii. 4.
BURNEY, Fanny (Madame d'Arblay), the *Essay* on, referred to, i. 184; her novels, i. 135, 296 and note.
BURNS Centenary in 1857, Macaulay's fifty reasons for not going to take part in, ii. 439.
BURY, Lady Charlotte, Brougham's article on, ii. 12.
BUTLER, Montagu, Fellow of Trin. Coll. Cam. (Head Master of Harrow), ii. 396.
BUTLER, S., author of *Hudibras*, ii. 291 and note.
BUXTON, Sir T. Fowell (1st Bart.), his amendment on the Slavery Bill of 1833, i. 314–316; 321; his letter to Z. Macaulay on the abolition of slavery, i. 316; in the smoking-room of House of Commons, i. 244.
BUXTONS, The, i. 131.
BYNG, "Poodle," i. 282, 343.
BYROM, John, his lines to Joanna Bentley in the *Spectator*, ii. 366 and note.
BYRON, Lord, his gift to Lady Holland, i. 219; at Florence, i. 223; uncared for by men, i. 223; publication of his poems, ii. 252; his poor powers of criticism, i. 221, 342; Macaulay's opinion of *Don Juan*, ii. 267; *alluded to*, i. 58 *sq.*, 121; ii. 29, 110, 395. See *Macaulay—Writings*.

Cabinet, A, noted for the University distinctions of its members, ii. 354; the making of in 1845, ii. 170 *sq.*; in December, 1852, ii. 339; Chatham and Macaulay quoted as to unanimity in, ii. 66.
"Cabinet Minister, The First," some unlucky words in a speech of Macaulay's, ii. 75 and note.
CADOGAN, 3rd Earl, ii. 57.
CÆSAR, Julius, how described by Aulus Gellius, i. 238*n*.; his remark to Brutus, i. 393*n*.; Cicero's estimate of his style, i. 449*n*.; Macaulay on character of, i. 467*n*., 477; his bust in the Vatican, ii. 33; his glory compared to Homer's, ii. 215; his *Commentaries*, i. 379, 449, 452, 477; his *Fragmenta*, i. 477.
Caffre War in 1851, ii. 205.
Calcutta. See *India*.
CALDERON, a favourite of Macaulay's, i. 263, 280, 468; ii. 285; *quoted*, ii. 482.
CALLIMACHUS, i. 452; ii. 437.
Calne, Macaulay offered the seat in Parliament for, i. 144; *alluded to*, i. 245, 262.

Cambridge, Macaulay at, i. 75–111 ; proud of his success at, ii. 437 ;
fond of famous students of, ii. 437; Union Society, i. 82; ii. 328;
a happy repartee at, i. 81; Parliamentary Election at, i. 75 ; the
Senate and Catholic Emancipation, i. 150; Macaulay's vists to,
i. 183; ii. 438; appointed High Steward of the Borough, ii. 439;
Barnwell Theatre at, ii. 214n.; Macaulay's list of the Senior
Wranglers, ii. 206 ; Modern History Chair, ii. 265; Chair of
Medicine, ii. 295 ; gardens at, ii. 401 ; college livings, ii. 437 ;
Bible Society of, ii. 439 ; ―― Trinity College, i. 75 sq., 85, 110 ;
Thirlwall and, i. 437, 438, and note ; Trinity Fellows, ii. 32, 182,
410 and note, 437 ; Macaulay's tutor at, ii. 329 ; his love for his
College, i. 77 ; ii. 410n.; audit ale, i. 181.
CAMDEN, Lord Chancellor, ii. 277.
CAMERON, C. H., one of the Indian Law Commissioners in 1835, i. 421 sq.,
431, 447, 468.
CAMOENS, Luis de, his *Lusiad*, i. 389, 458.
CAMPBELL, Alexander, candidate for Edinburgh in 1852, ii. 319.
CAMPBELL, Lord Chancellor, ii. 277, 366 and note, 441, 489 ; his *Lives*,
ii. 248, 277, 302.
CAMPBELL, Margaret, Macaulay's grandmother, i. 7.
CAMPBELL, Thomas, Poet, refers to Macaulay's *Political Georgics*, i.
232 ; proposes Buonaparte's health at a literary dinner, ii. 251n. ;
his writings, ii. 106 ; Macaulay's estimate of them, ii. 251 ; his
Life, by Beattie, ii. 251.
Canadian Insurrection in 1838, ii. 40, 117n.
CANNING, Lord, Governor-General of India, i. 435.
CANNING, Right Hon. George, his accession to power in 1827, i. 143 ;
Macaulay's oratory likened to his, i. 177; his saying about the
taste of the House of Commons, i. 179 ; Croker calls him " his
right honourable friend," i. 245n. ; one of the founders of the
Quarterly Review, ii. 242 ; Lawrence's portrait of, ii. 33 ; *alluded
to*, i. 193, 237, 316, 328 ; ii. 352, 381, 434, 466, 490.
CANNING, Sir Stratford (Lord Stratford de Redcliffe), i. 346.
CANTERBURY, Archbishops of, Macaulay repeats the list of, ii. 206 ; how
ranked by him, ii. 475.
Canton, i. 342 sq.
CAPEFIGUE's history of the Consulate and Empire of Napoleon, Macaulay's project of reviewing, ii. 81.
CARDIGAN, 7th Earl of, Macaulay defends him in Parliament, ii.
86 sq.
CAREY and HART, Messrs., American publishers, ii. 125n.
CARLILE, Richard, his infidel publications, i. 289.

CARLISLE, 7th Earl of (Lord Morpeth), extracts from his journal, ii. 196-203, 309; his mention of Prescott the historian in connection with Macaulay's MSS., ii. 229*n.*; his reference to Macaulay's conversation at a dinner at *The Club*, ii. 279*n.*; alludes to Macaulay's bad health in 1854, ii. 332; and in 1858, ii. 438; his account of a breakfast at Holly Lodge in 1856, ii. 412; his reflection on finishing Macaulay's *History*, ii. 454*n.*; at the funeral in Jan. 1860, ii. 489; was present at Canning's funeral, ii. 490.

CARLYLE, Thomas, meets Macaulay at Lord Ashburton's, i. 8; ii, 199*n.*; bored by the *Junius* question, ii. 199*n.*; *quoted*:—for his criticism on Croker's *Boswell*, i. 251*n.*; on the Reformed House of Commons, ii. 62; his description of Coleridge in *Sterling's Life*, ii. 470; his petition to Parliament on the Copyright question, ii. 135; a Knight of the Prussian Order of Merit, ii. 399*n.*

CAROLINE, Queen, the Macaulays partisans of, i. 101; Macaulay's Ode to, in 1820, i. 101.

Caroline, The, American steamboat, affair of in 1842, ii. 117 and note.

CASAUBON, Isaac, *quoted* in reference to the literary life, ii. 206, 359.

CASEMENT, Colonel, at Ootacamund, i. 386.

CASTI, author of *Giuli Tre*, ii. 27.

Castle Howard, ii. 49.

Cathedrals, tours to visit; Lichfield in 1849, i. 397*n.*; *various*, iii. 217, 263; Cologne and Strasburg, ii. 364 and note; Italian, ii. 416; Mrs. Stowe's account of Macaulay's remarks on, ii. 367 and note.

Catholics, Anglo-. See *Puseyitism*.

Catholics, Roman, cant of, ii. 291; Church of, in the early times, ii. 45; Manzoni's description of their Church, ii. 418; doctrine of Immaculate Conception, ii. 36; are the best of the native Christians in India, i. 383; payment of Irish priests, ii. 149-151; Mass-Book, ii. 23; Papal Bull of 1850, ii. 200*n.*; Macaulay's notions of a Catholic Peer of old family, ii. 31; *Emancipation*, i. 82, 154, 163, 172; Cambridge Senate petitions against claims of, i. 150; Wellington and the Relief Bill, i. 163*n.*; Brougham's jealousy on the subject of the Bill, i. 192; Macaulay alludes to, in Irish debate of 1833, i. 297 and note; Peel in relation to Catholic disabilities, ii. 465 *sq.*

CATULLUS, i. 452, 470; Greek excellence found in him alone of the Romans, i. 476; Macaulay touched by him as by no other writer, ii. 458 *sq.*

CECIL, W. (Lord Burghley), his compliment to Raleigh, ii. 231.

CERVANTES, his vein of ridicule like Plato's, i. 445.

Don Quixote, "the best novel in the world," i. 339, 361, 379, 389; ii. 329; *quoted*, ii. 253.
CHALMERS, Dr., Scotch theologian, i. 198, 418.
CHAMBERS, Dr., physician, i. 296.
CHANTREY (Sir Francis), sculptor, discovers a table of his own making at Rogers's, i. 231 *sq.*; meets Macaulay at dinner, i. 358; his sculptured children in Lichfield Cathedral, i. 397n.
CHARLES I. of England, *alluded to*, i. 185, 283, 290; ii. 362.
CHARLES II. of England, his remark on his portrait, ii. 16; Guizot's question about, ii. 396.
CHARLES X. of France, his coup-d'état, i. 171; victories of his reign illustrated at Versailles, ii. 49.
CHARLES XII. at Bender, i. 477.
CHARLOTTE, Princess, her death alluded to, i. 92 and note.
Charterhouse boys, well grounded in Greek, i. 436.
Chartists, The Welsh, Macaulay's letter on pardoning, ii. 180.
CHATEAUBRIAND, Z. Macaulay corresponds with, i. 66; Macaulay reads his *Génie de Christianisme*, ii. 418; his estimate of it, ii. 419.
CHATHAM, 1st Earl of, his fame not to be compared to Johnson's, i. 451; his simile of the Rhone and the Saône, ii. 19 and note; his saying about unanimity in Cabinets, ii. 66; *alluded to*, i. 342; ii. 368, 465.
CHATHAM, 2nd Earl of, ii. 413.
Chatsworth, i. 434.
CHATTERTON, Thomas, Southey's kindness to, ii. 469.
Chaucer, the Caxton editions of at Althorp, ii. 274; *alluded to*, i. 231, 476; *quoted*, ii. 228.
Cheddar Church, Somersetshire, the *Book of Martyrs* kept in, ii. 324, 326.
Chelsea Hospital, Chaplainship of, ii. 181.
CHELSUM, James, one of Gibbon's antagonists, ii. 289 and note.
CHEROKEES, i. 380; their language referred to by Macaulay in one of his Speeches, ii. 346n.
Chester, visited on an Easter tour, ii. 217 *sq.*
CHESTERFIELD, 4th Earl of, Macaulay's estimate of, i. 328 *sq.*, 342; his *Letters*, i. 327 *sq.*, 342 and note.
CHETWOOD, a Drury Lane prompter, his book about famous actors, ii. 132.
Chickasaws, i. 380.
Child's Own Book, The, a suggested prize-book for a Calcutta College, i. 418.

CHILDERS, Eardley, father of the statesman, i. 104 *sq.*
China, monopoly of the trade in 1833, i. 298 *sq.*; motion on the war with in 1840, ii. 75, 76*n.*; war with, in 1857, ii. 434*n.*, 440.
Cholera in London, 1831-1832, i. 229, 240, 264.
CHRIST, JESUS, the first great repudiator, ii. 197; Macaulay on the miracles of, ii. 200.
Christian Observer, The, edited by Z. Macaulay, i. 50 *sq.*, 62; Macaulay makes Index to 13th vol. of, i. 62; his letter on Fiction to, i. 62; "Excubitor's" letter in, i. 93; *alluded to,* i. 119.
Christianity, its phraseology in Latin, ii. 23; local traditions of, how far clear, ii. 45; at the period of Bulwer's *Pompeii,* ii. 46; on the hustings, ii. 59. See *India.*
Christians, of Tanjore, i. 383; in India, i. 386; their observation of the seventh day, ii. 336*n.*; the term Methodist applied to, i. 100.
Christmas in 1783 and 1852, ii. 339.
Chrysostom, Montfauçon's edition of, i. 473.
Church of England, The Established, wants men like Tillotson and Leighton, i. 438; Lord Derby's promises about, in 1852, ii. 312; Church fasts and feasts, ii. 409.
Church of Scotland, the Bill in 1853 for provision of the Edinburgh clergy, ii. 356 *sq.*
CIBBER, Colley, his Birthday Odes, i. 467*n.*; *alluded to,* ii. 368.
CICERO, Macaulay's advice to students on the study of, i. 84; his feelings towards his first Proconsul, i. 301*n.*; Macaulay much interested in character of, i. 448; his estimate of Cæsar's style, i. 449*n.*; the scene of his death, ii. 43; Macaulay's favourite work of, ii. 395*n.*; his estimate of powers of, ii. 395, 466; *alluded to,* i. 60, 91, 97, 300, 418, 431 *sq.*, 450-452, 456, 462, 470; ii. 248, 418 and note, 431.
City Companies, dinners of, i. 67*n.*, 343, 345.
Civil Service Reform, in 1853, ii. 380-384.
Clairvoyante at Bishop of Oxford's, ii. 310.
CLANRICARDE, Marchioness of, Canning's daughter, i. 236 *sq.*
CLANRICARDE, 1st Marquis of, ii. 139.
Clapham, Macaulay's childhood passed at, i. 27-29, 61-64; changed order at, i. 73; a picture-shop at, i. 374; the old church at, ii. 255; Macaulay tempted to buy a house at, ii. 403; *alluded to,* ii. 139, 297, 324.
Clapham Sect, The, i. 69-74; Stephen's article on, i. 69*n.*, 70*n.*
Claremont, Princess Charlotte's death at, i. 92.
CLARENDON, Edward Hyde, Earl of, historian; his *History,* i. 61, 339; ii. 138*n.*; his *Life* of himself, i. 339; *alluded to,* i. 380; ii. 115, 198.

CLARENDON (George Villiers), 4th Earl of, i. 270; at Cambridge, i. 78n., 80; his answer to Macaulay about Wellington and the Catholic Relief Bill, i. 163n.; at a consultation of Whigs, ii. 168, 171.
CLARKE, Longueville, "the O'Connell of Calcutta," i. 405, 459.
CLARKSON, Thomas, i. 91.
CLAUDE, painter, ii. 113.
CLEOPATRA, the cause of Cæsar's conduct in the Alexandrian affair, i. 477.
CLIFFORD, Lord, meets Macaulay at Rome in 1838, ii. 31 sq.
CLIFFORD, ———, *Times* reporter, his recollection of Macaulay in House of Commons, ii. 141.
Clifton, Macaulay at, ii. 216, 322–331.
Clitumnus, the white oxen of, ii. 29.
CLIVE, Lord, story of the lac of rupees, ii. 350, 351n.; *alluded to*, ii. 115. See *Macaulay—Writings*.
Clubs. See *London*.
COBBETT, William, speaks during the Irish Debate in 1833, i. 297; Macaulay's estimate of his powers, ii. 286n.; his abuse of all public men, ii. 299; likened to Latimer, ii. 475; his *Political Register*, i. 331; ii. 286 and note, 299, 455.
COBDEN, Richard, made an orator by "a course of mobs," i. 290; defeated at the General Election of 1857, ii. 440.
COCHRANE, Baillie, M.P., one of the "Young England" party in 1843, ii. 133.
COCKBURN, Lord, his *Journal* and *Memorials* quoted, i. 121, 143, 160, 192n., 198; ii. 184, 188.
Codes, Criminal ——— French, i. 423, 427, 468; Louisiana, i. 423, 427, 468; North German of 1871, i. 427. For Indian, see *India*.
Cold Bath Fields, "a broken head in," an apophthegm, i. 301n.
COLERIDGE, Derwent, college contemporary of Macaulay, i. 78, 80.
COLERIDGE, H. Nelson, college contemporary of Macaulay, i. 78, 80; on the staff of the *Etonian*, i. 117.
COLERIDGE, Samuel Taylor, Byron prefers Rogers and Gifford to, i. 342; his faculty of extracting the one bright thing out of dull matter, ii. 204n.; his criticisms on style, ii. 284; his *Ancient Mariner* an early favourite of Macaulay's, ii. 329; his talk recorded by Carlyle, ii. 470; *quoted*, ii. 251; for his estimate of Southey's character, ii, 426 and note.
COLERIDGE, Sara, i. 78; *quoted* for a remark about her father, ii. 204n.
"Collating Eye," the old scholar's, ii. 437n.
College contemporary of Macaulay, his guest at Clifton, ii. 326–328.
College life in London, ii. 94, 247.

COLLIER, Jeremy, his controversy with Congreve, ii. 80.
COLLINS, Anthony, Deist, his account of Voltaire, ii. 100n.
COLMAN, George, dramatist, i. 418; his *Broad Grins*, ii. 395.
COLMANS, The. See *Edinburgh Review*.
Cologne, ii. 364; Macaulay disappointed with the Cathedral, ii. 364n.
COLVIN, J. R., E.I.C.S., at Calcutta, i. 431.
COLYAR, ——, an English resident in Rome in 1838, ii. 31 and *note*.
Commissions, Royal, held in time of the Melbourne Ministry, ii. 60.
Comtism, *alluded to*, ii. 467.
Conscience, a novel, ii. 324.
Control, Board of. See *Macaulay—Miscellaneous Notes, Office*.
CONYBEARE, Rev. W. J., his criticism on Macaulay's *History*, ii. 250.
CONYBEARE, Mrs., Macaulay's cousin, *quoted* for reminiscences of him in Great Ormond Street, ii. 124, 139.
COOPER, Fenimore, his novel *The Pathfinder*, ii. 322n.
Coquette Corrigée, La, two famous lines in, i. 127 and note.
Corn-Laws, Macaulay's opinion in 1833 respecting the, i. 346; the crusade against in 1841, ii. 88; Lord J. Russell's motion about, ii. 89 *sq.*; the question of, at the General Election of 1841, ii. 92; Macaulay's conviction about total Repeal of, in 1845, ii. 174, 177, 188; the Bill passes the House of Lords in 1846, ii. 177. See *Anti-Corn Law League*.
CORNEILLE, i. 185.
Cornhill Magazine, the first number of, found by Macaulay's side at his death, ii. 488.
CORNWALL, Barry (B. W. Proctor), at a fancy ball in 1831, i. 227.
CORNWALL, William, on a college reading-party in 1821, i. 105.
CORNWALLIS, Lord, Macaulay's estimate of, ii. 115; his statue in Calcutta, i. 406.
Correspondents, Macaulay's Eccentric; — the Abbotsford letter, ii. 299; Crump's offer of 500 dollars, ii. 202; a fool's Impromptu on two histories, ii. 463; the painter's request for a cow, ii. 463; the schoolmaster's pamphlet on India, ii. 463; the Scotch clergyman, ii. 462; the novel-writer, ii. 463; the Wiesbaden poetaster, ii. 462; a New York Philosophical Society, ii. 203. *See* Applicants.
COTTENHAM, Lord Chancellor, ii. 168.
COTTLE, Joseph, Bristol bookseller, publisher of *Early Recollections of Coleridge*, ii. 426n.
Countries, discussion on the north and south of, with reference to literature, ii. 202.
COURTENAY, Peregrine, M.P. for Totness in 1831, i. 276.

COVENTRY, 1st Lord, Lord Keeper in 1625, ii. 439.
COWAN, Charles, candidate for Edinburgh in 1847, ii. 189 *sq.*; at head of the poll, ii. 191; his election in 1852, ii. 319; Macaulay's feeling for, ii. 337; *alluded to*, ii. 314.
COWPER, William, rendering of a word in his translation of Homer, i. 228; Macaulay's intimate acquaintance with, ii. 9; his autobiographical narrative, ii. 302; *alluded to*, i. 135; ii. 390, 408; *quoted*, i. 48, 58; ii. 486.
COXE, Archdeacon, his *History of the Pelham Ministry*, i. 391.
CRABBE, George, poet, a favourite of Macaulay's, i. 61; ii. 426*n.*
CRADOCK, J. H. (2nd Lord Howden), Wellington's A.D.C. in 1815, i. 213 *sq.*
CRAIG, W. Gibson, M.P. for Edinburgh in 1841, ii. 93; his regard for Macaulay, ii. 345; *alluded to*, ii. 81, 185, 195, 315 *sq.*, 319, 337, 344.
CRANMER, Archbishop, Macaulay severe on, at one of Rogers's breakfasts, ii. 198; a little hard on him in the *History*, ii. 237; less estimable than Gardiner, ii. 475.
Creole, The, mutiny of slaves on board, ii. 117.
Crichton, a novel, ii. 46.
Cricket-match between the Royal Engineers and the Zingari, ii. 355 and note.
Crimean War, Macaulay's interest in the, ii. 375–379, 379*n.*, 387, 390.
CROKER, Right Hon. J. Wilson, his attack on Brougham in 1830, i. 174; in the House of Commons, i. 245 and note, 254, 269; Macaulay's antipathy to, i. 128 *sq.*, 245, 254, 267; ii. 130, 468; his *Boswell's Johnson*, i. 233, 251 and note, 254; his answer to Macaulay's article, i. 255 and note; Carlyle on, i. 251 and note; his article in the *Quarterly Review* on the *History*, ii. 242 *sq.*, 257, 263.
"Crokerish Proceeding," a, ii. 101.
CROMWELL, Oliver, Macaulay's boyish opinion of, i. 32; High Steward of Cambridge, ii. 439.
CROPPER, Charles, Macaulay's nephew, to whom he had left his library, ii. 15 and note, 216 *sq.*
CROPPER, Edward, married Margaret Macaulay, i. 292, 307, 333, 355.
CROPPER, John, i. 292.
CRUMP, Mr., desirous of seeing his name in Macaulay's *History*, ii. 202.
CUBBON, Colonel, entertains Macaulay at Bangalore, i. 374.
CUMBERLAND, Duke of, in Scotland in 1745, ii. 40.
CURIONI, Signor, i. 211.
CURLL, Edmund, bookseller, ii. 372 and note.

CUTHBERTSON, Mrs. Kitty, her novels, i. 136.

DALHOUSIE, Lord, Commander-in-Chief in India in 1830-31, his cook, i. 429 and note.
DALY, Henry, i. 30.
DAMIENS, R. F., the assailant of Louis XV., i. 424.
DANDO, a hero of oyster shops about 1850, ii. 281 and note.
DANTE, Macaulay's early love for, i. 185 ; how ranked by him among the poets, i. 380 ; ii. 202; his great admiration of, i. 389; ii. 23; his reflections on seeing his monument in Florence, ii. 23 ; *quoted*, ii. 23.
DARLINGTON, Earl of (afterwards 2nd Duke of Cleveland), M.P. for South Shropshire, ii. 90.
DARU's *Histoire de Venise*, i. 390.
DARWIN, Charles, meets Macaulay at Chevening, ii. 413.
DAVIES, Dr. H. E., an antagonist of Gibbon, i. 470; ii. 289 and note.
DAVILA, Italian historian, i. 361, ii. 235 ; how ranked by Macaulay among historians, i. 458.
DAWSON, G. R., M.P. for Harwich in 1831, i. 269.
DECAZES, Duc, Talleyrand's mention of, i. 238.
DECIUS, Roman Emperor, ii. 268.
DEFOE, Daniel, Macaulay's youth nourished on, ii. 455 ; estimate of his powers as a writer, ii. 464 *sq.*; his *Robinson Crusoe* referred to, i. 28, 106, 336, 416, 418, ii. 286, 408*n.*, 464 ; other writings of, ii. 465.
DELANOUE, M., French comedy-writer, i. 127*n*.
DEMOSTHENES, Macaulay's admiration for, i. 457, 465 ; ii. 302, 419 ; his *De Coronâ*, i. 449, ii. 431 ; his statue in Rome, ii. 33 ; *alluded to*, i. 452 ; *quoted*, as to the power of oratory, ii. 75*n.*, for a rebuke to his brother ambassadors, ii. 369*n*.
DENISON, J. E., M.P. for South Notts in 1833 (Speaker 1857-1872), i. 242 *sq.*, 319.
DENMAN, Hon. Margaret, married to Macaulay's brother Henry, i. 313*n*.
DENMAN, Sir Thomas (Lord), his remark on one of Macaulay's Reform Speeches, i. 176 ; Brougham's feeling towards, respecting the seat for Calne, i. 158, 192; his daughter married to H. Macaulay, i. 313*n*.
Denmark, King Christian of, Lord Holland's account of, i. 278.
DERBY, Earls of. See *Stanley*.
DERBY family, The, and Preston races, ii. 185.
DERING, Sir Cholmeley, killed by Thornhill in a duel in 1711, ii. 116.

Derivations, a discussion on, at a breakfast party, ii. 201.
DERRY, the Bishop of, in 1832, i. 271.
Destiny, a novel by Susan Ferrier, i. 221.
DEVONSHIRE, Duchess of (Georgiana, wife of 5th Duke), verses of the, i. 328.
DEVONSHIRE, 6th Duke of, i. 250, 328.
DICK's *Moral Improvement*, i. 418.
DICKENS, Charles, Macaulay's opinion of, ii. 117, 122, 214; his writings —*American Notes*, ii. 117, 121; *Bleak House*, ii. 486; *Copperfield*, i. 2; ii. 214; *Dombey*, ii. 214; *Hard Times*, ii. 387; *Humphrey's Clock*, ii. 121; *Nicholas Nickleby*, ii. 161n.; *Pickwick*, i. 470 sq.; ii. 442 and note.
Dicky, Little, nickname given to Norris, an actor, ii. 131 and note, 132.
Dictionary, A Critical Pronouncing, i. 419.
DIODORUS SICULUS, i. 457, 465.
DISRAELI, Right Hon. Benjamin (Earl of Beaconsfield); his estimate of Macaulay in the *Young Duke*, i. 230 and note; his compliment to Macaulay's eloquence in the House of Commons in 1846, ii. 180; his amendment to the Address in 1849 on the subject of Palmerston's foreign policy, ii. 255; proposes Lord J. Russell's health at Academy Dinner in 1852, ii. 308; Macaulay approves his speech on Budget, in Dec. 1852, ii. 338; his Budget defeated, ii. 360; D.C.L. at Oxford in 1856, ii. 399n.; his *Coningsby*, i. 128; *Vivian Grey*, i. 346; *Young Duke*, i. 221, 230 and note.
Dissenters, their admission to Cambridge University proposed by Thirlwall, i. 438n.; Macaulay's considerateness for, ii. 126, 409; mentioned in his rhyming doggrel, ii. 209.
Distinctions, two, quoted by Macaulay from Sir J. Sinclair's writings, ii. 201.
Ditton Marsh, Macaulay at, ii. 387.
DOBREE, Peter Paul, Greek Professor at Cambridge, ii. 437.
Doctor, the quoting, i. 443n.
DORCHESTER, Lord, his scuffle with Buckingham alluded to in the *Edinburgh Review*, ii. 115.
DOVER, Lady, ii. 197n.
DOWNING, Mr., *Daily News* Reporter, his recollections of Macaulay in the House of Commons, ii. 143.
DOWTON, William, actor, ii. 294.
DRUMMOND, H., M.P. for West Surrey, ii. 345.
DRUMMOND, Mrs., Macaulay expresses in a letter to her his preference for Calcutta to Dublin, i. 433; he dines with her, ii. 202.

DRYDEN, John, his *Fables* how far fitted for ladies' reading, i. 94; three great dialogues in his Plays, ii. 279*n.*; Macaulay's intimate acquaintance with his works, i. 59, 122*n*, 190; ii. 9, 110; his reference to them in his speech on Copyright, ii. 137*n.*; Tonson's treatment of, i. 351.

Dublin. See *Ireland.*

Duchess, The, at Holland House, her distress about her sailor son, i. 324; her remark about Lady Morgan's harp, i. 325.

DU DEFFAND, Madame, *Letters* of, i. 362.

DUDLEY, Lord, his house in Park Lane, i. 436.

DUFFERIN, Lady (daughter of T. Sheridan,) her account to Macaulay of the Duchess of York's dogs at Oatlands, ii. 415*n.*

DUFFERIN, 4th Lord, and the magnetoscope, ii. 309.

Dukinfield, the working-men of, and Macaulay's *History*, ii. 239.

DUMONT, P. E. L., corresponds with Z. Macaulay, i. 66 *sq.*; welcomes Macaulay in Paris in 1830, i. 206.

Dunallan, a novel, i. 361.

DUNCANNON, Lord, M.P. (4th Earl of Bessborough), Teller in the Division of 22 March, 1831, i. 208; *alluded to*, i. 242 *sq.*, 357.

DUNCOMBE, Thomas, M.P. for Finsbury, his motion about the Chartists in 1842, ii. 183.

DUNDAS, Right Hon. H. (Lord Melville), successful in the House of Commons, i. 179; *alluded to*, i. 72, 154, 160; ii. 67, 184, 319.

DUNDAS, Sir David, M.P. for Sutherlandshire, dines at The Club, ii. 199; in the British Museum board-room with Macaulay, ii. 205; at a Holly-Lodge breakfast, ii. 412; a pall-bearer at Macaulay's burial, ii. 489; *alluded to*, ii. 315.

DUNGANNON, 3rd Lord (A. H. Trevor), his History of William III., ii. 107; mentioned as a bad writer of history, ii. 322.

Durham, visit to, ii. 218.

DURHAM, Dean of. See *Waddington.*

DURHAM, 1st Earl of, one of Lord Grey's Cabinet, 1831, i. 236; Governor of Canada in 1838, ii. 25; reference to his resignation, ii. 25 *sq.*; Macaulay's estimate of his powers, ii. 25; Brougham's remark on his Report, ii. 50.

EARDLEY, Sir Culling. See *Smith.*

Eastern Question in 1840, Macaulay's opinion on, ii. 82 *sq.*

EBRINGTON, Lord, M.P. for North Devon, Macaulay looks upon him as a possible leader of the Whigs in 1831, i. 199; *alluded to*, i. 242, 246; ii. 38.

EDEN, Hon. Emily, sister of the 2nd Lord Auckland, i. 137.

EDGEWORTH, Maria, the "second woman of her age," i. 246; her satisfaction at finding her name mentioned in Macaulay's *History*, ii. 238 and note; her *Absentee*, ii. 238n.; her *Patronage*, i. 222 and note; her *King Corny*, ii. 238n.; *alluded to*, i. 61, ii. 270.
Edinburgh, Macaulay's visits to, in 1828, i. 150, 153; in 1833, i. 305, 335, 391; in 1852, ii. 336 *sq.*; in 1859, ii. 482; his admiration of the old Town, i. 153, and of the view from Castle, i. 391; Sunday in, ii. 187, 336 and note; Philosophical Institution of, ii. 400; Macaulay's *political connection* with: — his election in 1839, ii. 64; re-election in 1839, ii. 70; in 1841, ii. 93; in 1846, ii. 178; in 1852, ii. 312-320, 330; religious ferment keeps him away from, in 1840, ii. 80 *sq.*; his unpopularity in, in 1847, ii. 151, 182-184; Radicalism in, ii. 183; a disadvantage of being its representative, ii. 156, 187; the 1847 election, ii. 189-191; 337; his defeat, ii. 191; reaction in his favour, ii. 195; his address in Music Hall, in Nov., 1852, ii. 334, 335n., 337; his wish to resign his seat, ii. 375; his resignation in 1856, ii. 402; question of the Established Church in, ii. 344, 356-358; *alluded to*, i. 149; ii. 439n., 466.
Edinburgh Review, The; "the blue and yellow," i. 245, 311; ii. 122; motto of, ii. 101 and note; a standing dish with the Macaulays, i. 61; Macaulay takes out a set to India, i. 362; his first public speech noticed in, i. 114; commencement of Macaulay's connection with, i. 120 *sq.*; lays the foundation of his social success, i. 181; editorship offered to him, i. 192; his pride in the connection, i. 205; cannot write much for it in 1832 and 1833, i. 262, 331; kept afloat in 1833 by his articles alone, i. 304; mention of payment for an article in, i. 311; the connection mutually beneficial while he is in India, i. 356; he objects to write on certain subjects in, ii. 8 *sq.*, 68, 121; cannot do much for it in 1843, ii. 127; his opinion on its functions as a Whig organ, ii. 151; the rumour in 1845 that he had ceased to write for, ii. 163; his last appearance in, in 1844, ii. 164n.; his influence over, well known in 1844, i. 70n.; he objects to appearance of his name in, ii. 13, 121; his style imitated in, ii. 462; Brougham's connection with, see *Brougham;* article on the Colmans, ii. 85; on Duelling, ii. 115 *sq.*; Empson, Editor of, ii. 16, 362; Jeffrey's connection with, see *Jeffrey;* Napier as Editor of, ii. 104; article on Niebuhr, i. 201; Number 101, i. 200; the Number for July, 1833, i. 321; and for April, 1838, ii. 11; proposed article on Penal Code of India, ii. 12 *sq.*; Stephen's article on the

Edinburgh Review, The (continued):—
  Clapham Sect, i. 70*n.*; Palmerston invited to write for, ii. 118;
  Macaulay wished to enrol Dickens on the staff of, ii. 122;
  recommended G. C. Lewis for the Editorship in 1852, ii. 362;
  alluded to, ii. 176, 362, 448.
Education Question, in 1839, ii. 68; Sir J. Graham's scheme, ii. 150
  and note.
ELDON, Lord, i. 114, 329.
Elections, Parliamentary, and religious worship, remark on, i. 289;
  Election Committees, oath taken by, ii. 47; general election of
  1874, i. 289.
Electricity and Table-turning in Macaulay's chambers, ii. 311.
ELIOT, George, author of *Adam Bede, quoted*, ii. 230, 244.
ELIOT, Lord, M.P. for Cornwall, ii. 78.
ELLENBOROUGH, Earl of, Governor-General of India, Macaulay's opposition to, ii. 138–141; his opinion on the Indian Civil Service Report of 1853, ii. 351–353; his motion on the Indian Mutiny, ii. 441 *sq.*
ELLESMERE, Lord (Lord Chancellor under James I.), High Steward of Cambridge, ii. 439.
ELLICE, Right Hon. Edward, M.P. for Coventry in 1832, i. 243.
ELLIS, Francis, son of T. F. Ellis, i. 209, 447, 468.
ELLIS, Marian, daughter of T. F. Ellis, ii. 236.
ELLIS, Mrs. T. Flower, i. 183, 345, 447, 468; ii. 52 *sq.*
ELLIS, T. Flower, Macaulay's familiar friend, i. 182 *sq.*; one of the
  Parliamentary Boroughs Commissioners in 1831, i. 253 and note;
  Macaulay's affection for, i. 345; ii. 415; his wife's death, ii.
  52 *sq.*; his ballads, ii. 95 and note; Recorder of Leeds, ii. 220*n.*;
  invited by Macaulay to the Isle of Wight in 1850, ii. 284 *sq.*;
  alluded to, i. 188, 200 *sq.*, 323, 361, 467; ii. 51–53, 100*n.*,
  172*n.*, 215, 233, 235 *sq.*, 247, 268, 328, 368, 395, 410*n.*, 448*n.*
ELPHINSTONE, 13th Baron, Governor of Madras, i. 54*n.*
ELPHINSTONE, Mountstuart, Governor of Bombay, ii. 53*n.*, 413.
EMERSON, R. W., American writer, ii. 277.
EMPSON, W., Editor of *Edinburgh Review*, his wish to notice the
  Indian Penal Code, ii. 12 *sq.*; Brougham's anger against, ii. 16;
  his last illness in 1852, ii. 362; *alluded to*, i. 128*n.*, 188; ii. 6,
  15, 44, 105.
Engineers, The Royal, their athletic pre-eminence, ii. 355; their
  famous innings in a cricket-match, ii. 355*n.*
England, its reactionary government 1790–1815, i. 159–162; the wish
  of the middle classes to make their sons gentlemen a curse of,
  i. 338; Macaulay's complaint about the youth of, in 1850, ii.

England (*continued*):—
258; his pride in her greatness, ii. 267; and grief caused by dangers that threaten her, ii. 447; Warren Hastings one of her greatest men, ii. 85.
English; conversation with Lady Holland about the purity of the language, i 213 *sq.*; Macaulay's Minute in 1835 about teaching, in India, i. 409 *sq.*; value of the language and literature to the natives of India, i. 410; state of literature in 1850, ii. 258; in 1855, ii. 392.
EPICTETUS, ii. 292.
Epicureans, their exaggeration on the subject of religious terrors, ii. 458.
ERSKINE, Lord Chancellor, not successful in the House of Commons, i. 179; his forensic ability, ii. 466.
ESSEX, 5th Earl of, i. 296, 343.
Eton College, Metcalfe and Wellesley at, ii. 352; Canning at, ii. 434.
Etonian, The, i. 117.
EURIPIDES, Macaulay's early dislike to, i. 440; his later admiration of, i. 456, 482; how he ranked the plays, i. 482*n.*; Brougham on the pronunciation of the name, ii. 260; not one of the six first-rate Athenians, ii. 433; Macaulay's proposed emendation in a passage in, ii. 437, 438*n.*; quotation from *Medea*, ii. 481; Croker's quotation of a corrupt passage in, i. 255 *sq.*; *alluded to*, i. 443, 452, 454, ii. 268.
Evangelical Party, organisation of, the work of the Clapham Sect, i. 69*n.*
EVANS, William, a defeated candidate for Leicester in 1826, i. 146.
EVANS, Sir De Lacy, M.P. for Westminster in 1852, ii. 319.
EVERETT, A. H., American writer, tells Macaulay of the success of his *History* in America, ii. 397; Macaulay's letter to, about the first volumes, ii. 398*n.*; *alluded to*, ii. 156, 196, 393.
Exeter, population in 1685, ii. 221.
Exeter Hall, *alluded to*, ii. 78, 150, 466.
Exhibition of 1851, Macaulay's pleasure in, ii. 210, 231, 298*n.*; the opening ceremony of, ii. 297; its closing, ii. 210.

Fainting-fits, number of in a certain novel, i. 136.
False quantities, the English horror of, ii. 201 *sq.*
Fancy-Ball, Macaulay's description of a, i. 225–227.
Fathers, The, Macaulay reads in India, i. 473; his opinion of them very like Gibbon's, ii. 40 and note; their authority settled for ever by Middleton, ii. 474*n.*
FAWCETT, John, actor, ii. 294.
FEARON, H. B., author of *Sketches of America*, ii. 117, 247.

FÉNELON's *Dialogues of the Dead*, i. 42.
FERGUSON, Sir R., M.P. for Londonderry, shows Macaulay over Londonderry, ii. 226.
FERGUSSON, Cutlar, M.P. for Kirkcudbright, i. 242*n*.
Ferney, Macaulay's visit to, ii. 100*n*.
FERRIER, Susan, her novels, i. 221, 282, ii. 302; *quoted*, ii. 410*n*.
FICINUS, Marsilius, i. 445.
FIELDING, Henry, i. 445, ii. 138*n*., 218; *quoted*, ii. 353 and note.
FINCH, Sir Heneage, ii. 439.
FITZCLARENCES, the, i. 210.
FITZWILLIAM, 4th Earl, dismissed from the Lord Lieutenantcy of West Riding of Yorkshire, i. 96; praised by Croker in House of Commons, i. 245*n*.; his unlucky quotation, ii. 201.
FITZWILLIAM, 5th Earl, High Steward of Cambridge, ii. 439. See *Milton, Lord*.
"Flashes of Silence," Sydney Smith's phrase quoted by Lord Carlisle, ii. 332.
FLAXMAN, John, his carved chimney-pieces at Rogers's, i. 231.
FLECKNOE, R., playwright, ii. 137*n*.
FLOOD, Henry, Irish patriot, his *Life*, ii. 267.
FLORUS (Annæus), i. 456.
FOLLETT, Sir W., M.P. for Exeter, ii. 61.
FONBLANQUE, Albany, editor of the *Examiner*, ii. 83; his leading articles re-published, ii. 113.
FOOTE, Samuel, actor and writer, ii. 250.
FORDS, The, Lord Carlisle's mention of in his Journal, ii. 202.
FORDYCE's *Sermons*, i. 361.
FORTEGUERRI, Italian romantic poet, i. 478.
Fourierism, social system invented by C. Fourier, ii. 467.
Fox's *Book of Martyrs*, the copy in the English College at Rome, ii. 32; the copy in Cheddar Church, ii. 327; and in Wrington Church, ii. 328.
Fox, Charles James, distinguished at school, ii. 381; greatly loved, i. 193, 223; story of Wilberforce and, i. 194 *sq.*; his duel with Adam, i. 240; his favourite play of Euripides, i. 482; his *History*, i. 328; Macaulay's eloquence likened to his, i. 177, 187, 235; portraits of, i. 217, 219; Macaulay compares his own face to his, ii. 278; *alluded to*, i. 161, 316; ii. 277, 388.
Fox, Henry. See 1*st Lord Holland*.
France, her "three days of July," i. 291; the National Guard in 1830, i. 170; Macaulay's visit to, in 1830, i. 166–171, 201; in 1838, ii. 18 *sq.*; in 1839, ii. 48 *sq.*; in 1840, ii. 82 *sq.*; in 1843, ii. 144–149; in 1858, i. 475; Blois, ii. 144; Rouen, i. 167.

FRANCIS, Sir Philip (supposed *Junius*), Mr. Tierney's opinion of, i. 190; his saying about Pitt, i. 193; story of Tierney and, i. 195; Macaulay on subject of *Junius*, i. 296; a discussion on, at one of Macaulay's breakfasts, ii. 199; Carlyle much bored by the subject at Lord Ashburton's, ii. 199*n.*; his tract on the *Blockade of Norway* in the style of *Junius*, ii. 290; *quoted*, ii. 6.

Frankfort, Macaulay visits Goethe's house at, ii. 302*n.*; the Museum at, ii. 428.

Fraser's Magazine, Carlyle's review of Croker's *Boswell* in, i. 251*n.*; J. Kemble's review of Macaulay's *History* in, ii. 451.

FREDERIC THE GREAT, his life and times as connected with English history, ii. 107; *alluded to*, i. 140, 415. See *Macaulay—Writings*.

Freeholder, The, a bi-weekly paper in 1715–16, ii. 455.

French :—Codes, i. 423, 468; eminent persons in 1858, ii. 442 *sq.*; Emperor of the, in 1858, ii. 443; society at commencement of First Empire, ii. 411; pamphlet sent to Macaulay in 1859 by M. de C——, ii. 376*n.*; manners of the provincial gentry in 1843, ii. 148; a people which must be despotically governed, ii. 443; discussion about the word *pudeur*, ii. 471*n.*; the prophet of the 17th century and Lord Holt, ii. 203*n.*; Republican sailors at Sierra Leone, i. 15–20; Revolution of 1830, i. 166, 259, 447.

FRESHFIELD, J. W., M.P. for Penryn, ii. 78.

Friendship's Offering of 1833, Macaulay's *Armada* first published in, i. 262.

FUSELI, Henry, painter and art-critic, ii. 210.

GAINSBOROUGH, Thomas, painter, ii. 331.

GARDINER, Stephen (Bishop of Winchester, Lord Chancellor of England), Macaulay's estimate of, ii. 474.

GARRICK, David, Jeffrey's face likened to his, i. 151; H. More's description of it, i. 151; *alluded to*, i. 265; ii. 294, 368, 490.

GEORGE, David, and his Baptists at Sierra Leone, i. 23.

GENLIS, Madame de, a favourite author of Macaulay's, i. 42, 134, ii. 100*n.*

Gentilshommes Chasseurs, Les, a book read in 1850 by Macaulay, ii. 279.

Gentleman's Magazine, Porson's letters to Travis first appeared in, ii. 293 and note.

GEORGE III., the subject of a debate at the Cambridge Union, i. 83; how his birthday was celebrated in 1832, i. 260.

GEORGE IV., his Irish expedition in 1821 discussed by Macaulay in a letter, i. 106 *sq.*; his death, i. 166.

German art, Macaulay criticises modern, ii. 430; a German knight,
i. 227 and note; Macaulay made Knight of the Prussian Order
of Merit, ii. 399.
German Theatre, in Macaulay's library, i. 186.
Gerundio, Fray, satirical romance by Father Isla, ii. 471.
GIBBON, Edward, his style affected, i. 456; a mistake of his, i. 468;
his answer to Davies, i. 470; his treatment of Christianity, ii. 40
and note; the style of historical essays considered relatively to
his, ii. 109; his *History*, ii. 138n.; not according to Macaulay's
conception of history, ii. 274; his antagonists, ii. 289 and note,
290; his answer to Warburton about the 6th Æneid, i. 470; ii.
395; *quoted*, for remark on society and Parliament, ii. 178; on the
"invincible love of reading," ii. 478; *alluded to*, i. 60, 361, 379,
418, 451; ii. 235, 395.
GIFFORD, William, poet and editor of *Quarterly Review*, Byron's estimate of, i. 342.
Gil Blas, an early favourite of Macaulay's, i. 60; ii. 46; a suitable
prize-book for a Calcutta college, i. 418; *Llamela* alluded to, i. 372.
GILMOUR, Mr., Macaulay meets at Londonderry in 1849, ii. 226.
GISBORNE'S *Duties of Women*, i. 361.
GLADSTONE, Right Hon. W. E., M.P.; in House of Commons, in 1833,
i. 303; his allusion to Z. Macaulay in the Sugar Debate of 1841,
ii. 89 *sq.*; his speech in December, 1852, ii. 338 *sq.*; an advocate
of Civil Service Reform, ii. 383; his eloquence likened to
Plunket's, i. 178; meets Macaulay in Rome, ii. 41, 52; his book
on Church and State, ii. 50 *sq.*; Macaulay's review of it, ii. 51,
53; his second work on same subject, ii. 79, 81; *alluded to*, ii.
366, 375, 390.
Glasgow, Macaulay presented with the freedom of, in 1849, ii. 261 *sq.*;
invited to the Burns Centenary at, in 1857, ii. 439n.; elected
Lord Rector of the University of, ii. 261, and delivers his address,
ii. 261.
GLEADALL, J. W., on a reading party with Macaulay in 1821, i. 105.
GLEIG, Rev. G. R., Chaplain-General to the Forces, his *Life of W.
Hastings*, ii. 84 *sq.*, 101; opening paragraphs of Macaulay's
review of, ii. 101 *sq.*
Glencoe, Macaulay's visit to, ii. 223, 282; his account of the massacre
of, ii. 231-233.
GLENELG, Lord. See *C. Grant*.
GLOUCESTER, Duke of, in the Chair at an Anti-Slavery Meeting in
June, 1824, i. 114, 116.
GODERICH, Lord, Prime Minister in 1827, i. 143. See *Ripon, Earl of*.

INDEX TO TREVELYAN'S LIFE OF MACAULAY. 29

GODWIN, William, *alluded to*, i. 311.
GOETHE, his *Wilhelm Meister*, ii. 8, 302, 304 ; his house at Frankfort, ii. 302*n.*; Macaulay's admiration of two lines of, ii. 22; his advice on the subject of writing a large work, ii. 448*n.*; *alluded to*, i. 461, 473; ii. 476.
Goezmans, the, and Beaumarchais, ii. 362, 363 and note.
GOLDSMITH, Oliver, his *Histories*, i. 417; his *Vicar of Wakefield*, i. 418; ii. 102 *sq.*; his *Poems*, ii. 367; *alluded to*, i. 221; ii. 490.
GORDIAN, Roman Emperor, i. 468.
Gorham case, the, in 1850, ii. 258.
GOULBOURN, Right Hon. Henry, M.P. (Chancellor of the Exchequer under Sir R. Peel), Macaulay talks with, on subject of Election Committees, ii. 47 ; *alluded to*, ii. 68, 367.
GOWER, Earl, i. 242.
GRAHAM, Sir James, M.P., his kind conversation with Macaulay on his Indian appointment, i. 354; his admiration of Hannah Macaulay for accompanying her brother to India, i. 358; his allusion to the Windsor Castle address in the House of Commons, ii. 74 ; his motion on the China war, ii. 75 *sq.*; his speech on the 4th June, 1841, ii. 91 and note ; his Education scheme in 1843, ii. 150 and note ; is attacked by Macaulay on the subject of opening letters at the Post-office, ii. 160; is pleased by Macaulay's success as an historian, ii. 245 ; congratulates him on the Edinburgh election of 1852, ii. 330 ; takes part in the debate about Sir C. Napier in 1854, ii. 378; *alluded to*, i. 234, 242 and note, 246, 324.
GRANT, Charles, Director of East India Company, i. 70*n*.
GRANT, Charles (Lord Glenelg), is entrusted with the keeping of Lady Holland's conscience, i. 264 ; introduces the India Bill of 1833, i. 299; his praise of Macaulay's speech of 10 July, 1833, i. 300, 317; Macaulay's feeling of loyal attachment to, i. 300; his advice to Macaulay about the Indian appointment, i. 333; Macaulay's remark on his health, i. 338 ; Macaulay's affection for him, i. 354 ; ii. 50; his regret at Macaulay's departure for India, i. 354 ; his resignation of Colonial Secretaryship in 1839, ii. 50 ; *alluded to*, i. 64, 151, 186, 248, 306, 318 *sq.*, 323, 339 *sq.*, 342, 345 *sq.*, 358 *sq.*; ii. 367.
GRANT, John Peter, in Calcutta with Macaulay, i. 431.
GRANT, Robert (Governor of Bombay), his Jewish Disabilities Bill, i. 163; wants some one to defend his place in the Government, i. 186 *sq.*; newspaper reports that Macaulay was to succeed him, i. 196; relations between him and his brother, i. 354 ; *alluded to*, i. 64, 151.

GRANVILLE, Countess, wife of 2nd Earl, ii. 299.
GRANVILLE, 1st Earl, his estimate of the poet Rogers, i. 221; his writings, i. 328.
GRANVILLE, 2nd Earl, succeeds Palmerston as Foreign Secretary in 1851, ii. 304; answers Lord Ellenborough on an Indian question in the House of Lords in 1858, ii. 442.
Grasmere Churchyard, Macaulay's visit to, ii. 481.
GRATTAN, Henry, his grave in Westminster Abbey, i. 316.
GRATTAN, Henry, M.P. for Wicklow in 1833, i. 297.
GRAY, Thomas, his praise of Thucydides, i. 449; *quoted*, i. 106; *alluded to*, i. 99, 476.
GREAVES, ——, schoolmaster at Clapham, i. 29.
GREAVES, ——, of Fulbourn, his prize at Trinity College, Cambridge, i. 86.
GREAVES's edition of Russell *On Crimes*, i. 426.
Greek; language, i. 410; lectures in 16th century, i. 414; literature, Macaulay's fondness for, i. 439 *sq.*; as compared with Latin literature, i. 473 *sq.*; orators, how Philip and Alexander felt towards them, ii. 198; people, skilled in arts and sciences, i. 439; poets, i. 441; Macaulay's reading, in India, i. 436 *sq.*; versification, i. 84; ii. 268, 288, 381; writers, present facilities of reading, ii. 433.
GREEN, ——, of Messrs. Longmans' house, ii. 248.
GREENWOOD, J., on a reading party with Macaulay, i. 105.
Greenwood Lodge, Ditton Marsh, Macaulay at, ii. 387.
GRENVILLE, Right Hon. G., ii. 381; his practice of economy with regard to office emoluments, ii. 421*n*.
GREVILLE, Charles, called "Punch," i. 282; discusses at breakfast the question of miracles, ii. 200; meets Macaulay on May 1, 1851, ii. 297; his surmise about Palmerston in 1852, ii. 312.
GREY, Countess, wife of 2nd Earl, i. 235, 267.
GREY, 2nd Earl, Prime Minister, 1830-34; his name highly respected in England, i. 163; becomes Premier, i. 174; sends for Macaulay in November, 1831, i. 190 *sq.*; his regard for Macaulay, i. 196, 236; is offered the Garter, i. 212, 306; at coronation of William IV., i. 250 : his resignation in 1832, i. 259; referred to in Macaulay's speech on Ireland in 1833, i. 297*n.*; his portrait, i. 218; in H. B.'s caricatures, i. 235; Macaulay's humorous description of, in 1833, ii. 197*n.*; *alluded to*, i. 194, 252, 273 *sq.*, 302, 320, 333, 340.
GREY, 3rd Earl (Lord Howick), i. 78, 235 *sq.*, 303; his connection with Lord J. Russell's attempt to form a Cabinet in 1845, ii. 171-176.

GREY, Lady Georgiana, i. 235.
GREY, Sir Charles, Member of *The Club*, ii. 53n.
GREY, Sir George, M.P. for Devonport in 1845, Macaulay looks to him as the future leader of the Whigs in the House of Commons, ii. 171; narrated to the Queen some of Macaulay's stories, ii. 295; at Windsor Castle with him, ii. 296.
GRIMM's *Correspondence*, i. 362, 390; ii. 100n.
GRINDAL, Archbishop of Canterbury, Macaulay's high opinion of, ii. 475.
GRISI, Madame, ii. 343.
Groans, a letter full of, ii. 145.
GROTE, George, his Ballot Bill and the Melbourne Cabinet in 1839, ii. 65; D.C.L. Oxford in 1856, ii. 399n.; the orthography in his Greek History distasteful to Macaulay, ii. 235; his *History* alluded to by Macaulay about Alcibiades, i. 453n.
Guardian, The, a daily paper in 1713, ii. 455.
GUICCIARDINI, Italian historian, how ranked by Macaulay, i. 458; the Essay on Burleigh *quoted* for reference to, ii. 239n.
Guildhall dinner in 1830, the, i. 173.
GUISCARD, Marquis de, Harley's assailant, i. 424.
GUISE, Duke of, in Blois Castle, ii. 144.
GUIZOT, François, French statesman and historian, in 1840, ii. 83; a refugee in 1849, ii. 197; Macaulay disliked his Ministerial policy, ii. 197n.; he praises Macaulay's *History*, ii. 197, 396; his question about Charles II., ii. 396; he tells Macaulay that he had proposed him as member of the Institute of France, ii. 399; Macaulay's criticism on his estimate of Peel, ii. 466n.
GURNEY, Hampden, Macaulay's remark to, on his own political creed, i. 79n.
GURNEY, Hudson, member of *The Club* in 1839, ii. 53n.
Gusman d'Alfarache, by Matteo Aleman, a Spanish romance of 16th century, referred to, by Macaulay, ii. 279n.
GUTHRIE, Dr., preacher and philanthropist, Macaulay attends his church in Edinburgh, in 1852 and 1859, ii. 336, 482.

H.B., political caricatures by, i. 235.
HADFIELD, George, M.P. for Sheffield, ii. 357 *sq*.
Haileybury College, ii. 380n., 382.
HALIFAX, Lord. See *C. Wood*.
HALL, Rev. Robert, his delight in Macaulay's Essay on Milton, i. 121.
HALLAM, Arthur, ii. 292; Tennyson's mention of, *quoted*, ii. 292n.

HALLAM, Harry, his death, ii. 292.
HALLAM, Henry, historian, at a breakfast party, ii. 196, 198, *sq.*, at *The Club*, ii. 279*n.*; brings home his dead son Harry, ii. 292; Macaulay visits him, ii. 292, 391, 405 and note; *alluded to*, ii. 156, 259, 307, 310.
HAMILTON, 4th Duke of, his duel with Lord Mohun in 1712, ii. 116.
HAMILTON, Mr., U.S., Macaulay meets at a breakfast party, ii. 196.
HAMPDEN, John, i. 98, 183. See *Macaulay—Writings*.
Hampton Court, ii. 387 *sq.*
HANKINSON, R., at school with Macaulay, i. 60.
HARDINGE, Lord, his story of Wellington, ii. 281.
Harfords of Blaise Castle, the, ii. 325.
HARPER, Messrs., of New York, publishers, alter the spelling of Macaulay's *History*, ii. 240.
Harrow School, a speech-day at, ii. 434.
HARVEY, Daniel Whittle, M.P. for Colchester, i. 271.
HASTIE, Mr., his bet about the sale of Macaulay's *History*, ii. 248.
HASTINGS, Warren, Macaulay thinks him one of England's greatest men, ii. 85, 115, 352; Gleig's *Life of*, ii. 84 *sq.*, 101 *sq.*; *alluded to*, ii. 67, 140. See *Macaulay—Writings*.
HAURANNE, Duvergier de, M., ii. 307, 443.
HAVILAND, I., Professor of Medicine at Cambridge, ii. 295.
HAWKINS, J. H., M.P. for Tavistock, i. 246, 249.
HAWKINS, Sir John, his Life of Johnson, i. 233.
HAWKINS, Vaughan, Fellow of Trinity College, Cambridge, ii. 396.
HAYDON, B. R., his picture of the Reform Banquet, i. 323; his *Memoirs*, ii. 363; Macaulay's estimate of, ii. 363.
HAYLEY, W., poet and biographer, i. 153; ii. 386.
HAYTER (Sir George), paints Macaulay for picture of the House of Commons, ii. 16.
HAYTER, Sir W. G., M.P. for Wells, Liberal Whip, ii. 339, 360.
HAZLITT, W., his application to himself of a quotation from Shakespeare, ii. 8.
Headlong Hall, a novel by Peacock, ii. 304*n.*
HEBER, Bishop, *alluded to*, i. 272, 383, 434.
HELIODORUS, i. 465; his *Æthiopics*, i. 466*n.*
HENDERSON, actor, on the dialogue in 4th Book of *Paradise Lost*, ii. 268.
HENDERSON's *Journal of a Residence in Iceland*, a favourite breakfast book with Macaulay, ii. 476.
HENRY IV. of France, his wish for every French peasant, i. 91.
HENRI V., son of Duc de Berri, ii. 144.
HERODIAN, ii. 326.

INDEX TO TREVELYAN'S LIFE OF MACAULAY. 33

HERODOTUS, Macaulay on the merit of a translation of, i. 380; his opinion of, ii. 247, 274, 277; *alluded to*, i. 437, 452, 455; ii. 241, 391, 470.

HERRIES, Right Hon. J. C., M.P., i. 208, 269.

HESIOD, i. 469, ii. 336n.; Macaulay's reference to, in his sorrow for his sister's death, i. 439 and note.

HILL, Matthew Davenport, M.P. for Hull, his connection with the Sheil affair in 1834, i. 364–366.

HILL, Rowland, visit of a Quaker uncle of Macaulay to his chapel, i. 21; stories of, ii. 199.

HIRTIUS, Cæsar's friend and writer of the *De Bello Alexandrino*, i. 477.

"History, Dignity of," ii. 110.

HOBBEMA, a fine picture by, at Mr. Littleton's, i. 242.

HOBHOUSE, Sir J. C. (Lord Broughton), i. 221; ii. 200, 316; retires from the Board of Control, ii. 305.

HODSON, Mr., of Cambridge, i. 42.

HOGARTH, W., his picture the *Lady's Last Stake*, ii. 430n.

HOLBEIN, his portraits of Wolsey and More, ii. 33.

Holland, Macaulay's tour in, ii. 157–160.

HOLLAND, Dr. (Sir Henry), Miss Edgeworth's letter to, about Macaulay's *History*, ii. 238; he compliments him on the 3rd volume of it, ii. 394; *alluded to*, i. 324; ii. 199, 201, 291 *sq.*, 479, 489.

HOLLAND, Henry, son of Dr. Holland, ii. 479.

Holland House, Macaulay describes his first visit to, i. 212–214; a breakfast at, i. 217 *sq.*; the grounds of, 219 *sq.*; he sleeps there and meets Talleyrand, i. 237; a distinguished party at, i. 273; is asked to live there almost entirely, i. 280; story of a Duchess at, i. 324 *sq.*; *alluded to*, i. 193 *sq.*, 215, 240, 264, 278, 280 *sq.*, 428.

HOLLAND, Lady, introduced to Macaulay, i. 210; conducts him over Holland House, i. 218 *sq.*; invites him to take up his quarters there, i. 280; her civility to him, i. 181, 214, 220, 235, 241, 324; praises his eloquence, i. 235; and his writings, i. 264, ii. 98; displeased with his essay on *Walpole*, i. 337, 347; her remarks on English language, i. 213 *sq.*; on Talleyrand, i. 238; her dream, i. 218; fear of cholera, i. 240, 264; scene with Macaulay about his going to India, i. 360; wants him to review her husband's "Protests," ii. 86n.; her gift to him, ii. 100; her behaviour to Allen and others, i. 214, 241, 274; at Rogers's dinner, i. 347; her request to Macaulay respecting his notice of Lord Holland in the *Edinburgh Review*, ii. 116 *sq.*; *alluded to*, i. 266, 273, 281, ii. 156.

HOLLAND, 1st Lord, epithet applied to, by Macaulay, i. 338; his grandson's opinion of, i. 338*n.*; Brougham objects to Macaulay's estimate of, ii. 98; his diary, ii. 156.

HOLLAND, 3rd Lord, Macaulay's regard for, i. 281; his character, i. 213 *sq.*, 220, 240 *sq.*, 281; at home, i. 217 *sq.*, 274, 325; like C. J. Fox, i. 241; on the subject of Macaulay's going to India, i. 360; his stories;—of Wilberforce, i. 194; of King Christian, i. 278; of Bp. Horsley, i. 324; his remark about 1st Lord, i. 338*n.*; approves of the essay on *Walpole*, i. 347; death, ii. 80; his "Protests," ii. 86*n.*; Macaulay's notice of his public speaking, ii. 116 *sq.*; a humorous description of by Macaulay, ii. 197*n.*; *alluded to*, i. 236; ii. 100; his sister, i. 282.

Holly Lodge, Macaulay's last home, ii. 403 *sq.*; described, ii. 406–408; hospitality at, ii. 409–412; his fondness for, ii. 17; *alluded to*, ii. 435, 458 *sq.*, 486–489.

HOLMES, Oliver Wendell, Dr., on the Indian Mutiny, ii. 445.

HOLT, Lord, Chief Justice of the King's Bench in 1689, story of, ii. 203*n.*

HOMER, inscription from at Holland House, i. 219; discussion about translation of a word in, i. 228 *sq.*; how ranked among poets ancient and modern, ii. 202 *sq.*; Macaulay strongly moved by reading, ii. 214 *sq.*, 300 and note, 431; early translations of, into Persian and Indian languages, ii. 472; *alluded to*, i. 91, 361, 379; ii. 203, 238*n.*, 336*n.*

Hong-Kong baker named A-lum, ii. 434*n.*

HOOK, Theodore, Macaulay's estimate of his writings, ii. 45, 468; *alluded to*, i. 307; ii. 286.

HOOK, Walter F., D.D., Vicar of Leeds, ii. 220 and note.

HORACE, his criticism of Æschylus, i. 437; Macaulay's explanation of the abrupt transition in the Odes, i. 440 *sq.*; his panegyric on the general Nero, i. 480; *alluded to*, i. 361, 379; ii. 29; *quoted*, i. 437*n.*, 442, 443*n.*, 446; ii. 272, 365.

HORNER, Francis, M.P., corresponds with Z. Macaulay, i. 66; *alluded to*, ii. 381.

HORSLEY, Bishop Samuel, of St. David's and St. Asaph, his dictum about the laws and the mass of the people, i. 162; Lord Holland tells stories of, i. 324.

HOTHAM, 3rd Baron, his motion about the Master of the Rolls, ii. 341–345.

Howard, Castle, Lord Carlisle's seat, ii. 49.

HOWARD, Charles, son of 6th Earl of Carlisle, ii. 200.

Howard family, Macaulay's acquaintance with the, ii. 196*n.*

Howard Shield, the, ii. 412.

HOWICK, Lord. See *Grey*.

HOWLEY, W., Archbishop of Canterbury, i. 138; at coronation of
William IV., i. 250.
HUDSON, Mr., of the East India House, Macaulay's letter to on the
advantages of a town life, i. 57.
HUMBOLDT, Baron von, communicates to Macaulay his nomination to
the Prussian Order of Merit, ii. 399.
HUME, David, his *History*, i. 418, ii. 138n.; Charles Lamb's remark
about, ii. 36n.; how advertised in 1849, ii. 258; Macaulay not
quite satisfied with his conception of history, ii. 274; his fame
superior to a politician's, i. 451; as a metaphysician, ii. 248;
quoted, ii. 362n.
Hungarian Brothers, The, a novel, i. 284.
Hungerford, Lord, the steamship which brought Macaulay home from
India, i. 473, ii. 1, 281.
HUNT, Leigh, Macaulay thinks he might succeed Southey as Laureate, ii.
85; his article in the *Edinburgh Review* on the Colmans, ii. 85;
agitated by Napier's letter to him, ii. 103-105; his idea of writing
on Mdme. d'Arblay, ii. 111; his criticism on the *Roman Lays*,
ii. 125; his sentiments on the subject of money, ii. 486; the
Harold Skimpole of *Bleak House*, ii. 486; in Newgate, ii. 332.
HUNT, H., M.P. for Preston in 1831, known by the title "Orator,"
i. 97.
HUNTINGDON, Lady. See *Methodists*.
HUNTINGTON, W., his religious confessions, ii. 302.
HURD, Bishop, Warburton's letters to, ii. 475.
Hyde Park on May 1, 1851, ii. 297.

INCHBALD, Mrs., her *Simple Story*, ii. 32.
INDIA:—unfamiliarity of its name in 1833, i. 335; Civil Service in
early part of 19th cent., i. 161; its high prestige at present day,
i. 430; renewal of Company's Charter in 1813, i. 44, 298, 403;
Bill of 1833, i. 298-301, 306n., 310, 317 *sq.*, 323, 326 *sq.*, 330,
340; ii. 346; Macaulay's great interest in Indian affairs, i. 261;
Indian politics, i. 263, 374; a "noble field for a statesman,"
i. 352; Macaulay nominated to Supreme Council, i. 330 *sq.*,
339 *sq.*, 344, 348; his appointment, i. 350, 355; preparations for
voyage, i. 348 *sq.*, 358; his object in going out, i. 382; bitterness
of his exile, i. 432, 478; ii. 392; on the voyage, i. 349, 358,
368 *sq.*, 379; ii. 287; lands in India, i. 370.
MACAULAY'S WORK IN INDIA:—utility of his labours, i. 420;
their advantage to himself, ii. 77; his conciliatory spirit, i. 412.
I. *Black Act*, i. 402-408, 455; ii. 372. II. *Penal Code*, i. 421-

INDIA (*continued*):—
427, 447, 463, 468, 472, 474 and note; ii. 12 *sq.*, 44, 447. III.
Education Minutes; of 2nd Feb. 1835 (Orientalist Question),
i. 409-412; ii. 372*n.*; various Minutes, i. 413-419. IV.
Censorship of the Press, Papers on the, i. 397-402.
HIS LIFE IN INDIA:—Visit to Arcot, i. 373; ii. 271; to Bangalore, i. 374.—Calcutta, i. 355, 376, 389, 391; club, i. 389, 459; factions in, i. 432; Government House, i. 389; habits in, i. 428-430; 436, 465, 469; his health, i. 435, 442, 450, 454, 460, 468; ii. 280; house and garden, i. 389, 428, 436; lawyers in, i. 459; newspapers, i. 399 *sq.*, 471; ii. 13; the O'Connell of, i. 459; parsons, i. 429; public opinion in, i. 404; public meetings, i. 405-407; records of his life in his classics, i. 469; society in, i. 359, 430 *sq.*; the Thirlwall of, i. 453; Wilson, Bishop, house of, i. 370.—Madras, barber at, i. 54*n.*; legislative wisdom at, i. 380.
—Mysore, i. 375, 377, 389.—Neilgherries, i. 376, 382-389; ii. 18.—Nepaul, i. 470.—Ootacamund, i. 369, 376, 378-389.—
Oude, i. 414.—Seringapatam, i. 9, 374.—Tanjore, i. 383.—Todas, the, i. 383.—Travancore, i. 9, 30, 36, 263.

VARIOUS:—An Indian bore the worst bore, i. 263; Christianity in, i. 30, 44, 383, 386, 413, 464; ii. 442, 446; the best of Civil Servants, ii. 352; climate of India, i. 358, 454; effect of education on Hindoo religion, i. 464; a classical examination, i. 453; the two best Governors-General, ii. 352; Hooghly College, i. 415; households in, i. 350; Hyder Ali, i. 375; income necessary for, i. 358; justice in, i. 387 *sq.*; Indian letters, i. 266; liberty in, i. 404; libraries, college, i. 414; literature, vernacular, in, i. 419; the Lucknow Resident, ii. 156-158; the Company's rule about maid-servants, i. 349; Nabobs, i. 371; a puppet-show, i. 463; a lac of rupees, ii. 351*n.*; a "sanaterion," i. 377; schools in, i. 416 *sq.*, 464; slavery in, i. 463; Swartz's people in, i. 383; Tippoo Sahib, i. 31*n.*, 374 *sq.*; titles in, i. 262; C. Trevelyan's report on transit duties, i. 392; the Zenana, i. 414.

Indian subjects after Macaulay's return home:—Civil Service Bill of 1853, ii. 346-356; Civil Service Committee, ii. 380 and note; Report of, ii. 380-382, 388; Mutiny in 1857, i. 372*n.*, 426; ii. 435 and note, 441-448; Macaulay much affected by the Indian troubles in 1857, ii. 447; Lord Ellenborough's motion for papers on, ii. 441 *sq.*; Lord Shaftesbury's petition, ii. 442.

INGLIS, Sir R. H., M.P., his judgment on Macaulay in society when young, i. 125; on the Reform Bill as first introduced, i. 175; *alluded to,* i. 131, 306; ii. 53, 281, 307.

Inscriptions, the rival merits of Latin and Greek, ii. 196.
Invisible Gentleman, The, a novel, i. 311.
Ireland, Macaulay's tour in, ii. 224-226, 267-271 ; Dublin, i. 433, 453, ii. 269 ; Killarney, ii. 270 and note ; Londonderry, ii. 224-226.
Irish :—Church Temporalities Bill in 1833, i. 298, 308, 470; Church property, four years' contest in Parliament over, ii. 58 ; Catholic priests, Macaulay's views on payment of, ii. 150; peasants, ii. 271*n*.; Bills in 1840, 1841, dealing with registration of voters, ii. 76 *sq.*; Croppies, ii. 120.
IRVING, Edward, an instance of an extravagant orator, ii. 210, and of a discarded favourite, ii. 252*n*.
IRVING, Washington, on first hearing the nightingale in England, ii. 22; *alluded to*, ii. 393.
ISOCRATES, i. 465 ; ii. 393, 433.
Italy, tour in, in 1838, ii. 16-48 ; in 1856, ii. 416-418 ; olive-trees in, ii. 22, 43 ; Clitumnus, ii. 29 ; Florence, ii. 21-28, 44 ; Genoa, ii. 20 ; Milan, ii. 416 ; Mola di Gaeta, ii. 42 ; Naples, ii. 44-46 ; Pisa, ii. 21 ; Pontine Marshes, ii. 42 ; Rome, ii. 29-42 (see *Rome*) ; Soracte, ii. 29 ; Thrasymenus, ii. 29 ; Venice, ii. 416 *sq.*; Verona, ii. 417 *sq.*
IVORY, Lord, his mention of the Edinburgh "disgrace" of 1847, ii. 337.

Jack the Giant-killer, of more use to school-boys than grammars of rhetoric and logic, i. 417 ; a reminiscence of, in the notes to the Penal code, i. 423.
Jacobites and the word "Limp," ii. 223*n*.
JACQUEMONT, Victor, his *Letters*, i. 390 ; his saying about Lord W. Bentinck, ii. 79.
JAMES I., *History of* (by Wilson), i. 60.
JAMES II. and Queen Victoria, Macaulay's remark on, ii. 279.
JARRATT, R. and T., on a reading party with Macaulay in 1821, i. 105.
JEBB, J., Bishop of Limerick, his edition of Burnet's *Characters*, i. 390.
JEFFREY, Francis (Lord), entertains the Macaulays in 1817, i. 67 ; described by Macaulay in 1828, i. 150-153 ; visited by Macaulay in 1849, ii. 262 ; as Editor of the *Edinburgh Review*, i. 121, 129, 191 *sq.;* his own articles, ii. 129, 152 *sq.*, 272 ; Brougham's feeling towards him, ii. 16 ; his opinion of Brougham, i. 193 ; his story of Macaulay's memory, i. 53*n*.; on Macaulay's style of writing, i. 122 ; on Macaulay's eloquence, i. 198 ; knows Macaulay's powers of criticism, ii. 8 ; on the *History of England*, ii. 235-237 ; Macaulay's opinion of his powers, ii.

JEFFREY, Francis (*continued*):—
9 *sq.*, 152 *sq.*, 278; not trained in Greek and Latin versification, ii. 381; his daughter, ii. 16*n.*; his death, ii. 277 *sq.*; letters to Napier, i. 357, 462.
JEFFREYS, Judge, alluded to by Macaulay in speech of 10th March, 1846, ii. 180.
JEKYLL, J., M.P., one of the wittiest men of his time, i. 179.
JEROME, St., Middleton's treatment of his writings, ii. 473*n.*
JESSE's *Selwyn Correspondence*, ii. 391.
Jesuit morality tested in Pascal's Letters, ii. 199, 471.
Jews:—petition for Removal of Disabilities of, i. 156; Macaulay makes his maiden speech on the Disabilities Bill, i. 163 *sq.*; frequent use of the olive as an illustration in their writings, ii. 22; their tact with regard to Pagan scholars as depicted by Philo, ii. 471.
JOHN, King, alluded to by Macaulay in a speech at Leeds, i. 290.
JOHNSON, James, hatter, his rhyming advertisement, ii. 366.
JOHNSON, Samuel, Dr., his commendation of Kenneth Macaulay's *St. Kilda*, i. 5; he visits him at Calder, i. 6; he meets Macaulay's grand-father at Inverary, i. 6 and note 7; story of the pretty goats and, i. 216 and note; the Prospectus to his Dictionary, i. 329; his letter to Lord Chesterfield, i. 329; Macaulay gets his *Life* as a school-prize, i. 419; his fame greater than Chatham's, i. 451; his first work, ii. 137*n.*; his epitaphs on Philips and Levett, ii. 199; Macaulay owns to a sympathy with some tricks of his, ii. 202; autograph of his *Irene*, ii. 400; Macaulay's article on in *Encycl. Brit.* quoted, ii. 241; Macaulay's sentence about his literary verdicts, ii. 430; his *Lives*, i. 418; ii. 137*n.*, 251; *alluded to*, i. 40, 134, 187, 237; ii. 9, 368, 490; *quoted:*—his love of a good hater, i. 128; excision of fine sentences, i. 155; "wretched, unidea'd girls," i. 190*n.*; his sentence about H. More, i. 233*n.*; on Akenside, i. 341; about thanks for favourable criticism, ii. 126; his judgment on the mutton, ii. 146; "working doggedly," ii. 272, 385; on round numbers, ii. 397; his own idleness lamented, ii. 453; the essential qualification of a biographer, ii. 457 and note.
JONES, Ernest, Chartist, alluded to by Macaulay in an Edinburgh speech, ii. 335*n.*
JONSON, Ben, the autograph of his *Masque of Queens*, ii. 400; *quoted*, ii. 390.
JOSEPHUS, ii. 471.
JOWETT, Rev. B. (Master of Balliol College), ii. 380*n.*, 395.

JUNIUS. See *Francis*.
JUSTINIAN, Pandects of, i. 454.
JUVENAL, some lines of his declaimed by Johnson, i. 7; *alluded to*, ii. 409.

KANT's works translated, Macaulay cannot understand, ii. 247.
KEAN, Edmund, ii. 294.
KEATS, John, i. 142.
KEITH of Ravelstone, Mrs., her remark to Scott about Afra Behn, ii. 465n.
KEMBLE, J. M., ii. 265; reviews Macaulay's *History* in *Fraser's Magazine*, ii. 451 *sq*.
KEMPSON, E., on a reading-party with Macaulay in 1821, i. 105.
KEN, Bishop, ii. 218.
KENNETT, Dr. White, Bishop of Peterborough, a bad writer of history, ii. 322.
KENNY, C., Dramatic author, i. 336.
KENT, Duchess of, Macaulay dines at her house, i. 309.
KERRY, Lord, son of 3rd Marquis of Lansdowne, i. 157.
KING, ——, Cambridge tutor in 1818, i. 90.
KING, Lord, i. 264.
KING, Mrs., author of *Female Scripture Characters*, i. 361.
KINGLAKE, A. W., ii. 259; *quoted*, for estimate of Lord Cardigan, ii. 86.
KNIGHT, Charles, his *Quarterly Magazine*, i. 117-120; ii. 123, 328, 460.
KNOX, John, i. 433.

LA FAYETTE, Marquis de, Commander of the National Guard in 1830, i. 169; Macaulay attends a soirée at his hotel in Paris, i. 171.
LA HARPE, J. F. de, his quarrel with Voltaire, ii. 100n.
LABOUCHERE, Right Hon. H., M.P. for Taunton, Lord of the Admiralty in 1832, i. 279, 353; ii. 171.
LAMARTINE, Alphonse de, his merit as a historian discussed, ii. 199.
LAMB, Charles, i. 424; on Hume and Smollett's *History of England*, ii. 36n.
LAMB, Hon. G., M.P., brother of Lord Melbourne, i. 241-243.
Lancaster, Macaulay on circuit at, i. 148; ii. 324.
LANDSEER, Sir E., R.A., ii. 430.
Lansdowne House, Macaulay at, i. 210, ii. 253; *alluded to*, i. 215, 240, 243.
LANSDOWNE, Lady, wife of 3rd Marquis, i. 157.

LANSDOWNE, 3rd Marquis of, his offer of Calne to Macaulay, i. 143 *sq.* 158, 192; talks to him about taking office in 1832, i. 195 *sq.*; on the Reform Bill in 1831, i. 252; meets him at Lord J. Russell's in 1852, ii. 339 *sq.*; conversation on Brougham, ii. 441*n.*; Macaulay's *Letters* to him; on going to India, i. 350-353, 367; on the House of Lords, ii. 59; on the subject of Prof. Owen's position at British Museum, ii. 449; at Ferney, ii. 100*n.*; his admiration of *Macbeth*, ii. 203; the Quakers and, ii. 253; Macaulay's affection for, i. 367; ii. 299, 488*n.*; *alluded to*, i. 81, 156-158, 210, 272; ii. 199, 372. See *Bowood.*

Laponian New Testament, ii. 384.

LARDNER, Dr. Dionysius, i. 226; his dealings with Sir J. Mackintosh, i. 351; Macaulay writes for his *Cabinet Cyclopædia*, i. 172.

LATIMER, Bishop, ii. 289*n.*; "the Cobbett of the Reformation," ii. 475.

Latin, the finest lines in the language, i. 379; its use during the revival of letters, i. 410; the worst written book in ancient, i. 466; the most eloquent passages in, i. 467; not really suited for the phraseology of Christianity, ii. 24; prose writing, Macaulay's advice as to, i. 84; versification, ii. 381.

Laureateship, Poet, an absurd fashion, ii. 86.

Laurie Todd, a novel, by Galt, i. 221.

LAWRENCE, Abbott, American minister in England in 1852, ii. 308.

LAWRENCE, Dr., M.P., a noted wit, i. 179.

LAWRENCE, Sir Thomas, his portrait of Fox, i. 217; his sketch of Boswell, i. 233; his portrait of Mrs. Littleton, i. 242; of Wellington and of Canning, ii. 33.

LEACH, Captain, at Londonderry in 1849, ii. 224.

LEADER, N. P., M.P., i. 273*n.*

Leeds, Macaulay asked to stand for as its first Member, i. 258; his canvass in 1832, i. 284-292; the election, i. 294 *sq.*; farewell address to the electors in 1834, i. 363 and note; population of in 1685, ii. 220 *sq.*; *alluded to*, i. 112, 262, 279, 282, 325.

Leeds Coach, the children in the, i. 280.

LEFEVRE, Sir J. Shaw, at college with Macaulay, i. 90; on the Indian Civil Service Committee of 1854, ii. 380*n.*; at a dinner of ex-Fellows of Trin. Coll. Cambridge, given by Macaulay, ii. 410*n.*

Leigh Court, near Clifton, collection of pictures at, ii. 330..

LEIGH, Pemberton, at a dinner at *The Club*, ii. 279*n.*

LEIGHTON, Archbishop of Glasgow, i. 438.

LEO THE GREAT, Gregory XVI. likened to, ii. 32.

LEONARDO DA VINCI, ii. 230 *sq.*

LESSING, i. 473; Macaulay's admiration of his *Laocoon*, ii. 8 and note, 470.
Letters, revival of in Europe, i. 410.
LEWIS XIV. See *Louis XIV*.
LEWIS (Right Hon. Sir), G. Cornewall, M.P., ii. 201; Macaulay recommends him for editorship of *Edinburgh Review* in 1852, ii. 362; a pall-bearer at Macaulay's funeral, ii. 489.
LEWIS, M. G., "Monk," Macaulay's estimate of, ii. 386; *alluded to*, ii. 415n.
Liberals, an union of, suggested by Joseph Hume in 1852, ii. 376.
Lichfield, Macaulay at, in 1849, i. 397n.; ii. 218.
LIEVEN, Madame de, her letter to Greville about the Exhibition of 1851, ii. 297.
LINDSAY, Lady C., daughter of 8th Lord North, her account of an incident in the riots of 1780, i. 302 *sq.*; Macaulay dines at her house, ii. 259.
LINGARD, Dr., new edition of his *History*, and Macaulay's first two volumes, ii. 243.
LISTER, Mrs. (Lady Theresa), sister of the 4th Earl of Clarendon, i. 270, 272.
LISTON, John, actor, ii. 294.
Literary Gazette, Editor of, offers to defend Macaulay about Penn, ii. 232.
LITTLE's poetry, the poems in *Knight's Quarterly Magazine* likened by Z. Macaulay to, i. 118.
LITTLETON, E., M.P., 1st Lord Hatherton, Macaulay dines with, i. 242; *alluded to*, i. 240, 309 *sq.*, 319.
LITTLETON, Mrs., wife of preceding, her beauty, i. 240, 242, 309, 323; pays Macaulay a compliment on his profile, i. 323.
LIVERPOOL, Earl of, Prime Minister 1812–1827, i. 82, 102; ii. 91.
Liverpool, Mr. Cropper's house near, i. 292.
LIVINGSTONE, Edward, his Code for Louisiana, i. 423, 427, 468.
LIVY, Macaulay greatly admires, i. 445, 479 *sq.*; *alluded to*, i. 452, 476, ii. 447.
Llanrwst, N. Wales, college reading-party at, in 1821, i. 105 *sq.*
LLOYD, J., on a reading-party with Macaulay in 1821, i. 105.
LOCKE, John, ii. 248; his urn at Barley Wood, ii. 326; his note-book in the British Museum, ii. 400; his *Essay on the Human Understanding*, ii. 138n.
LOCKHART, J., Editor of *Quarterly Review*, i. 390; objects to Croker's review of Macaulay's *History*, ii. 257; his *Life of Scott*, ii. 8 *sq.*, 455, 472; his translation of Spanish Ballads, ii. 278.

LONDON, agitation in, in Nov. 1830, i. 173; Macaulay's fondness for, i. 58; ii. 14, 287; his good knowledge of, i. 131, 189, 289; rambles in the City, i. 26, 131, 138; ii. 10, 97, 207, 232, 331; College life in, ii. 247; forecast about, ii. 31; few antiquities in, i. 167; a wish concerning, ii. 202; Bookstalls. See *Macaulay — Misc. Notes.*

Spots in London associated with Macaulay's name :—Albany, ii. 94, 99, 103, 170, 172n., 198, 247, 332, 390, 403 *sq.*; Birchin Lane, i. 26; ii. 420; Cadogan Place, i. 129, 326, 355; Clarges Street, ii. 7; Drapers' Garden, i. 26; Exeter Hall, *see* separate heading; Gray's Inn, i. 142; Great George Street, ii. 73, 99, 324; Great Ormond Street, i. 130 *sq.*, 133 and note, 137 *sq.*; Grillon's Hotel, political club at, i. 279; Holly Lodge, ii. 17, 403, 406–412, 435, 458 *sq.*, 488 *sq.*; Lock Chapel, i. 132, 243, 268; St. John's Chapel, i. 132, 302.

Clubs :—Athenæum, i. 168, 195, 230, 272, 336, 385; ii. 232, 243, 247, 339, 393n., 452, 467, 485n.; Brooks's, i. 243, 343, 367; ii. 175, 292, 304, 315, 319, 341, 384; Reform, ii. 175; The Club, ii. 53 and note; White's, i. 195, 328.

Various Localities :—Albion Tavern, i. 343; Bond Street, i. 190; Brunswick Square, i. 190, 274; Burlington Arcade, i. 167; Charing Cross, i. 451; the Clarendon Hotel, ii. 94; Cork Street, i. 190; Downing Street, i. 302, 452; Fleet Prison, i. 451; Green Park, i. 231; Grosvenor Place, i. 242; Hanover Square, ii. 213; Houndsditch, ii. 31; Hyde Park, ii. 297; Knightsbridge, i. 270; Lansdowne Place, i. 190; London Bridge, i. 343; Mecklenburg Square, i. 274; Palace Yard, i. 452; Park Lane, i. 436; Peacock Inn at Islington, i. 280; Regent Street, i. 167; Russell Square, i. 302, 355; St. Paul's, ii. 33; Spitalfields, i. 346; Turnham Green, ii. 307; Westbourne Terrace, ii. 232n.; Westminster Abbey, i. 249 *sq.*, 316, 326, 434n.; ii. 3, 22, 489 *sq.*; Westminster Hall, i. 434n.; ii. 106; Westminster School, i. 38; ii. 168, 352; Whitechapel, i. 346; Whitehall, i. 189.

Sights in :—British Museum, ii. 205, 216, 248, 264, 400, 449 *sq.*, 485n.; Chinese Museum, ii. 215; Colosseum, ii. 216; National Gallery, ii. 33, 217; Soho Bazaar, i. 168; Tower, ii. 216; Tussaud's, ii. 216, 258 *sq.*; Waterloo, Panorama of, ii. 216; Zoological Gardens, ii. 216, 259.

London idolatry, ii. 251 and note.
London servants in 1831, i. 242.
LONDONDERRY, 3rd Marquis of, his *Travels*, ii. 119.
LONG, George, Professor, at college with Macaulay, i. 84; i. 226.

INDEX TO TREVELYAN'S LIFE OF MACAULAY. 43

Longinus, i. 474.
Longleat Hall, Wilts, ii. 218.
Longman, Messrs., Publishers, i. 255, 390; the £20,000 cheque preserved among their archives, ii. 420.
Longman, Mrs., ii. 236.
Longman, Thomas, ii. 100, 236, 362, 372, 391, 419, 483.
Longman, William, ii. 252.
Longus, Greek sophist, his *Pastoralia*, i. 465.
Loughborough, Lord Chancellor, ii. 277.
Louis XIV. (spelt Lewis), described in Macaulay's college essay, i. 87 *sq.*; ii. 471*n.*; (spelt Louis), his bedroom at Versailles, ii. 49; William III.'s hatred of, ii. 198.
Louis XV., wounded by Damiens, i. 424.
Louis XVI., i. 159; (spelt Lewis), ii. 362.
Louisiana, Code of, i. 423, 427, 468.
Love Match, The, ii. 391.
Lubbock (Sir J. W.), 3rd Bart., Macaulay meets him at dinner, i. 296.
Lucan, Macaulay's admiration of, i. 54, 466, 467 and note; *alluded to*, i. 448, 452; ii. 437; *quoted*, i. 466 *sq.*
Lucca, Duke of, i. 373.
Lucian, i. 391, 452, 474; ii. 247, 357*n.*, 368, 431.
Lucretius, i. 452, 476; ii. 202, 458; *quoted*, i. 439, 444.
Lushington, (Dr.) Stephen, M.P., i. 271, 345 *sq.*
Luther's New Testament, i. 473.
Luttrell, Henry, a man of wit and fashion, author of *Advice to Julia*, i. 218, 220, 232, 273, 278, 359.
Luttrell, Narcissus, *Diary of*, 222*n.*, 223*n.*
Lyndhurst, Lady, i. 123.
Lyndhurst, Lord Chancellor, makes Macaulay a Commissioner of Bankruptcy, i. 143; *alluded to*, ii. 57, 59.
Lyon, ——, at Mr. Preston's school with Macaulay, i. 41.
Lyrical Ballads, The, ii. 329.
Lytton, 1st Lord. See *Bulwer Lytton*.
Lyveden, Lord. See *Smith, Vernon*.

Macarthy, Sir Charles, murdered by the Ashantees, i. 187.
Macartney, General, Lord Mohun's second in his duel with the Duke of Hamilton in 1712, ii. 116.
Macaulay and Babington, firm of, i. 37, 129.
Macaulay, Alexander, uncle of Macaulay, i. 8.
Macaulay, Aulay, Minister of Tiree and Coll, great-grandfather of Macaulay, i. 5 *sq.*

MACAULAY, Aulay, Rector of Rothley, i. 8 ; ii. 435.
MACAULAY, Charles, brother of Macaulay, i. 61, 225-227, 352; his brother's private secretary, ii. 73 ; his rambles in the City with his brother, ii. 97.
MACAULAY, General Colin, uncle of Macaulay, i. 8 *sq.*, 31 and note; 36 *sq.*, 68, 348, 374, 459; ii. 31, 419.
MACAULAY, Fanny, sister of Macaulay, i. 61, 210, 272, 310; ii. 2, 145, 200*n.*, 208, 216, 259 and note, 260, 395.
MACAULAY, Hannah More (Lady Trevelyan); *quoted* for mention of her brother:—Clapham, life at, i. 61 ; Macaulay as a boy, i. 67-69 ; a failure at Cambridge, i. 86; Great Ormond Street, life in, i. 131-133; his love for bad novels, i. 136; Calne offered to him, i. 143 *sq.*; visit to Cambridge, i. 183 ; on the subject of pecuniary troubles, i. 313; his feeling about scenery, ii. 17 *sq.*; his dread of separation in 1839, ii. 72, in 1859, ii. 479, 483 ; his distaste for society and love of children, ii. 206 *sq.*; on their Easter tours, ii. 217 ; on his elevation to the peerage, ii. 435 *sq.*; Scotch tour in 1859, ii. 481 *sq.*; his last days, ii. 487 ; her loss, ii. 489; her love for the Great Ormond Street home, i. 61, 133 ; resolve to go to India, i. 335, 358 *sq.*; on voyage, i. 369; in India, i. 389; her engagement to marry, i. 391-397, 435 ; in India, i. 430, 434, 439, 450, 460 ; move to Clapham, ii. 99 ; to London, ii. 232*n.*; at Clifton, ii. 322, 330 ;—*alluded to:* i. 133 *sq.*, 148, 191, 195 *sq.*, 292, 309 ; ii. 98, 234 *sq.*, 250, 273, 278, 291, 297, 316, 345, 367, 390, 395, 404, 427, 461*n.*
MACAULAY, Henry, brother of Macaulay, i. 61, 313 and note.
MACAULAY, Henry, son of preceding, i. 313*n.*
MACAULAY, Jane, sister of Macaulay, i. 45, 59 *sq.*, 91, 206.
MACAULAY, Jean (Mrs. Babington), i. 8, 22, 25.
MACAULAY, John, Minister of Inverary, grandfather of Macaulay, i. 6 and note, 7, 9.
MACAULAY, Rev. John, brother of Macaulay, i. 60, 103, 268, 311, 431*n.*; ii. 264.
MACAULAY, Joseph, nephew of Macaulay, i. 313*n.*
MACAULAY, Kenneth, author of the *History of St. Kilda*, i. 5 *sq.*
MACAULAY, Margaret, sister of Macaulay (Mrs. E. Cropper), his close companionship with, i. 133 ; her engagement to E. Cropper, i. 292 ; her death, and Moultrie's poem on, i. 396 and note ; i. 438 *sq.*, 481*n.*; ii. 427*n.*; her Journal, i. 185-197, 261 ; *quoted* for mention of Macaulay, i. 122, 127; *alluded to*, i. 61, 131, 183, 221, 274, 295, 307, 333 *sq.*, 355, 371, 381, 397*n.*; ii. 15.
MACAULAY, Misses, Macaulay's visits to them at Brighton, ii. 259*n.*

MACAULAY, Mrs. Zachary (Selina Mills), her engagement, i. 21 *sq.*;
her marriage, i. 25; her early treatment of her son, i. 33 *sq.*;
a letter to him, i. 45 *sq.*; her reading aloud, i. 61; her death,
i. 189, 206; her interest in her son's childish successes, i. 234;
alluded to, i. 26 *sq.*; ii. 146, 303.

MACAULAY, Selina, sister of Macaulay, i. 44 *sq.*, 60, 91, 355; ii. 235.

MACAULAY, THOMAS BABINGTON, LORD MACAULAY.
  i. Leading Events of his Life, see page 45 of this Index.
  ii. Miscellaneous Notes, page 48.
  iii. Personal Characteristics, page 48.
  iv. Mental and Literary Characteristics, page 49.
  v. His Work as a Writer, and a List of his Writings, page 51.
  vi. His Speeches, and Characteristics as a Speaker, page 55.
  vii. His Remarks, Opinions, Sentiments, page 56.
  viii. Letters written by him,[1] page 57.

(Reference may also be made to the following headings for allusions to Macaulay : America; Anecdotes; Applicants; Brougham; Cambridge; Correspondents; Edinburgh; Edinburgh Review; Holland, Lady; India; Jeffrey; Lansdowne; London; Macaulay, Hannah; Macaulay, Zachary; Palmerston; Parliament; Rogers; Smith, Sydney; Wilberforce, William.)

i. LEADING EVENTS OF HIS LIFE.

1800. Birth, 25th October, i. 25.

1803. His parents move to Clapham, i. 27; "while still the merest child" a day-scholar at Mr. Greaves's, i. 29.

1807. Visit to H. More at Barley Wood, i. 34 *sq.*, 35*n.*; ii. 303.

1813. To school at Little Shelford, i. 39.

1814. School moved to Aspenden Hall, Herts, i. 51; makes the index to the 13th vol. of *Christian Observer* at Christmas, i. 62.

1816. His letter on novels in 15th vol. of *Christian Observer*, i. 62.

1817. Tour in Scotland; entertained by Jeffrey, i. 67.

1818. Goes into residence at Cambridge, i. 75; his parents move to Cadogan Place, i. 129.

1819. Prize for English poem, *Pompeii*, i. 93.

1820. Prize for Latin Declamation, i. 84.

1821. Craven University Scholarship, i. 84, 436; prize for English poem, *Evening*, i. 83; joins a reading-party in Wales, i. 104.

---

[1] Not including extracts from letters.

MACAULAY (Lord), *continued:*—
1822. Prize for the Greaves Essay on William III., i. 86–88; takes his B.A. degree, i. 86.
1823. Takes pupils at Cambridge, i. 110, 130; writes for *Knight's Quarterly Magazine,* i. 117–119; ii. 123. His parents move to 50, Great Ormond Street, i. 130.
1824. Fellow of Trinity College, i. 85, 110; Speech at an Anti-Slavery Meeting at Freemasons' Tavern in June, i. 114.
1825. Begins to write for *Edinburgh Review,* i. 120.
1826. Called to the Bar, i. 112.
1827. Commencement of friendship with T. F. Ellis, i. 182.
1828. Commissioner of Bankruptcy, i. 143, 215, 220, 227.
1829. Consulted by Jeffrey on subject of editorship of *Edinburgh Review,* i. 192; takes chambers in South Square, Gray's Inn, i. 132, 142.
1830. Enters Parliament as Member for Calne, i. 143; his maiden speech, i. 163; re-elected for Calne, i. 166; first visit to the Continent, i. 167.
1831. Commissionership of Bankruptcy abolished, i. 180; the first of his Reform Speeches, 2nd March, i. 175; ii. 375; invited to stand as the first M.P. for Leeds, i. 258.
1832. Commissioner of Board of Control, i. 260; Secretary of the Board, i. 292; M.P. for Leeds in December, i. 294.
1833. Offers to resign office on account of West India Bill, i. 314, 316, 318, 320, 351; appointed to the Council of India, i. 350.
1834. Sails for India, 15th February, i. 367; lands in June, i. 369.
1835. Recommends the removal of the Censorship of the Press, i. 397; President of the Committee of Public Instruction, i. 408, 412; Minute on Education, 2nd February, i. 409; President of the Jurisprudence Commission, i. 421.
1836. Various Minutes on the Black Act, i. 403–405; State Paper on the Calcutta Press, i. 400.
1837. 2nd January, Minute on the Penal Code, i. 423; Report and Notes upon the Penal Code, i. 423.
1838. Leaves India in January, i. 435, 473; reaches England in June, ii. 1; tour in Italy, ii. 16–49; refuses the Judge-Advocateship, ii. 27, 38, 44.
1839. M.P. for Edinburgh, ii. 64; Secretary-at-War, ii. 69; re-elected for Edinburgh, ii. 70; begins to write *History of England,* ii. 69*n.*; elected member of *The Club,* ii. 53.

INDEX TO TREVELYAN'S LIFE OF MACAULAY. 47

MACAULAY (Lord), *continued* :—
1840. In office, ii. 73 *sq.*; in Great George Street, ii. 73.
1841. Re-elected for Edinburgh in the new Parliament, ii. 93, 95 ; resignation of Government, ii. 97 ; takes chambers in the Albany, ii. 94, 99.
1842. Publication of the *Lays of Ancient Rome*, ii. 122.
1843. Publication of the *Essays*, ii. 126; tour in France, ii. 144-149.
1844. His last appearance in the *Edinburgh Review*, ii. 164*n.*; tour in Holland, ii. 157–159.
1845. Letter to Mr. Macfarlan on the failure to form a Whig Ministry, ii. 173–175.
1846. Return of the Whigs to power; appointed Paymaster-General, ii. 177 ; re-elected for Edinburgh, ii. 178.
1847. Defeated in the contest for Edinburgh, ii. 191; appointed a Trustee of the British Museum, ii. 248, 400, 449 *sq.*
1848. Rector of Glasgow University, ii. 261 ; publication of Vols. I. II. of the *History*, ii. 236.
1849. Inaugurated as Rector at Glasgow, ii. 262 ; Professorship of Modern History at Cambridge offered to him, ii. 265 ; visit to Ireland, ii. 267–269.
1850. Appointed a Bencher of Lincoln's Inn, ii. 277 ; Professor of Ancient Literature to the Royal Academy, ii. 307*n.* ; at Ventnor, i. 475; ii. 284–286.
1851. At Malvern, ii. 300 *sq.*
1852. Asked to join the Whig Cabinet, ii. 305 ; elected M.P. for Edinburgh, ii. 319 ; commencement of bad health, ii. 320–322 ; at Clifton, ii. 322-331 ; Address at Edinburgh in November, ii. 334.
1853. His last Speech in the House of Commons, ii. 358 ; at Tunbridge Wells, ii. 368 ; preparation of his Speeches for publication, ii. 371 *sq.*; tour up the Rhine, ii. 364 ; receives various foreign distinctions, ii. 399.
1854. Chairman of the Indian Civil Service Committee, ii. 380 ; President of the Philosophical Institution of Edinburgh, ii. 400.
1855. Publication of Vols. III. IV. of the *History*, ii. 392.
1856. Resigns his seat in the House of Commons, ii. 403 ; D.C.L. at Oxford, ii. 399; moves to Holly Lodge, ii. 406; tour in Italy, ii. 416–418.
1857. Raised to the Peerage, ii. 434 ; High Steward of Cambridge, ii. 439 ; on the Indian Relief Committee, ii. 446; tour up the Rhine, ii. 407, 429, 435.

MACAULAY (Lord), *continued:*—

1858. Inaugurated High Steward of Cambridge, ii. 439; tour in France, i. 475.
1859. Tour to English Lakes and in Scotland, ii. 481-483; death, 28th December, ii. 489; burial, 9th January, 1860, ii. 489.

ii. MISCELLANEOUS NOTES :—Bar, his practice at the, i. 112, 144-155, 157, 427n.; his birthdays, i. 481; ii. 18 and note, 272, 291, 447; bookstalls, his knowledge of, i. 361; ii. 96n. 97, 132, 233, 324, 331; bored but once in his life, i. 384; loses his boyish tone, i. 293; one of the calamities of his happy life, ii. 174n.; carriage-keeping, ii. 296; *Favourites*, certain of his :—cities, i. 391; ii. 21, 337; historical characters, i. 467n.; ii. 21, 30, 85, 352, 475; English statesman, ii. 254; people, i. 249, 281, 302; ii. 254, 282, 316, 318, 413; 488n.; a picture, ii. 430n.; health, mention of bad, ii. 280, 317, 319-321, 343, 360, 375, 385-387, 438, 485-487; (for good health in India, see *India*); "marry, unlikely to," i. 460; *see* i. 394; one of his "greatest misfortunes," ii. 294; money matters :—income at various times, i. 143, 180 *sq.*, 311, 331, 343, 381, 442, 444, 459; ii. 28, 167, 171, 186, 208, 330, 365, 391, 419-422; no wish for great wealth, i. 331, 343, 352, 434, 460; ii. 27, 38, 103, 392; office, in, i. 260, 262, 280, 292, 320, 330, 351, 354; ii. 73 *sq.*, 177, 421; official life, dislike to, ii. 38, 172; Politician, as a :—early interest in public affairs, i. 69; not reared a Whig, i. 69, 79n.; his political views and opinions, i. 97, 125, 195, 199, 213, 252, 254, 285-287, 305, 308, 346, 352; ii. 167, 188, 248, 376; political life, indifference to, i. 309, 450, 474n.; ii. 305, 330, 440; cost of his elections, ii. 95, 178; Parliamentary seats offered him after 1847, ii. 195, 248 *sq.*; his advice on the formation of the Aberdeen Ministry, ii. 340; likened to Strafford, i. 455; to Blucher, ii. 340; seniors, a favourite with his, i. 157, 182.

iii. PERSONAL CHARACTERISTICS :—*Appearance and dress*, described by Carlyle, i. 8; in *Knight's Quarterly Magazine*, i. 122; by Crabb Robinson, i. 126; in *Blackwood*, i. 244; in a New York paper, ii. 210; *variously*, i. 123, 188, 424; ii. 204, 279n., 431; dress and toilet, i. 28, 54n., 68, 122 and note, 123, 188, 324; ii. 145 *sq.*, 149, 158, 210; manner and tone, i. 124, 293; ii. 204 *sq.*; portraits of him, i. 323; ii. 16, 278 *sq.*; statue at Cambridge, i. 123; castle-building, love of, i. 189; ii. 461 and note; dislike of charlatanism and affectation, ii. 201n., 235, 296, 310 *sq.*, 311n., 429, 467; of Abolitionist cant, i. 24n.; of Puseyitism, ii. 182,

INDEX TO TREVELYAN'S LIFE OF MACAULAY. 49

MACAULAY (Lord), *continued:*—
200*n.*, 201*n.*, 208, 256, 258, 290 *sq.*; childhood, his, i. 26, 28 *sq.*,
33 *sq.*, 40, 68; ii. 214*n.*, 303, 329, 460; children, fondness for,
i. 186, 465; ii. 27 and note, 207, 214, 216, 281, 291, 331, 413,
415, 428; contempt, prone to, i. 148 *sq.*, 228 *sq.*; ii. 464; correspondence, with his father, i. 139; character of his later, ii.
361; courage, i. 127; ii. 6; dogs, dislike of, ii. 414, 415*n.*; *see*
ii. 281; epicurean element in virtue, fond of an, ii. 276; family
affection and filial love, i. 98, 104, 119, 130, 140, 234, 293 *sq.*,
310, 313, 327, 346, 352, 381, 463, 465; ii. 250, 252, 333, 345,
425, 427, 447, 480; games and pastimes, fondness for certain, i.
131, 139, 185, 187; ii. 218, 233, 281, 483; gastronomic tastes,
i. 67*n.*, 80, 126, 157, 181, 213, 243, 246, 296, 305, 327, 343,
345, 348, 382, 389, 428–430, 434, 453, 463; ii. 14, 28, 45 *sq.*, 94,
145, 158, 200, 208, 210, 216, 247, 285 *sq.*, 291, 329, 332, 387,
404, 409, 410 and note, 411 *sq.*, 425, 436, 448 and note, 482;
water-drinking, i. 131; habits, daily, i. 188, 262, 280, 339, 428,
454, 465; ii. 247, 285, 332; kindness of disposition, i. 186, 350;
ii. 111, 126, 273, 275, 279, 299, 337, 387, 392, 409, 415*n.*, 425,
435, 445, 447, 480; liberality, i. 130, 313, 352, 381; ii. 147,
185, 252, 259, 275 *sq.*, 290, 298 *sq.*, 311*n.*, 323, 331, 385, 388,
394, 409, 422–424, 432, 456, 488; life, enjoyment of, i. 220, 384;
ii. 72, 75*n.*, 98, 174*n.*, 175, 207, 264, 278, 280, 286 *sq.*, 291,
294, 317, 333 *sq.*, 363, 389, 395, 435; music, no taste for, i.
137, 210 *sq.*, 455; ii. 295*n.*; Nature, beauty of, feeling towards,
i. 388, 466; ii. 17 *sq.*, 29, 268, 270*n.*, 285, 326, 364; love of
rivers, ii. 19 and note, 29, 144, 217, 326, 331, 388, 407; patriotism, i. 20, 73, 252; ii. 42, 267, 305, 375 *sq.*, 378, 444; sensibility
and emotionableness, i. 127, 293, 295, 302, 325, 388, 397*n.*, 445;
ii. 23, 27, 30, 53, 147, 149, 214 and note, 215, 281, 283, 292,
300*n.*, 306, 321, 323, 331, 333, 404, 418, 427, 431, 447 *sq.*,
458, 480 *sq.*, 483 *sq.*, 486–488; sight-seeing, theatres, etc.,
love of, i. 211, 215; ii. 46, 210, 214 and note, 215 *sq.*, 294,
295*n.*, 297, 298 and note, 306, 429 *sq.*; society, distaste for, i.
61, 182, 185, 305, 378, 430, 444, 463; ii. 187, 206, 244, 275,
299, 413, 476; sports, no sympathy for, i. 123 *sq.*, 373, 393; ii.
186, 270 *sq.*, 295, 357, 472; (for quoit-playing, *see* i. 107;) walking powers, i. 124; ii. 300; women's beauty, admiration of, i.
237, 240, 242, 250, 270, 302, 309, 323, 325, 360; women, various
notices of, i. 153, 246, 267, 360, 383, 430; ii. 15, 130, 157, 181,
369, 415*n.*
    iv. MENTAL AND LITERARY CHARACTERISTICS:—Acquirements,

MACAULAY (Lord), *continued :—*
the secret of his, i. 52. Conversational Powers—as a child, i.
28, 33 *sq.*, 48; in later life, i. 80 *sq.*, 124 *sq.*, 182, 186, 196,
243, 292, 311, 428; appearance and bearing in conversation, ii.
204; testimony of others, i. 124 *sq.*, 389; ii. 184, 198 *sq.*, 201*n.*,
203*n.*; at Buckingham Palace, ii. 280. Educational Instructor,
as an, ii. 431. Intellectual Strength, ii. 453; his one intellectual
vice, i. 405. Languages, learning, i. 188, 263, 339, 361, 389,
439, 458, 461, 469, 473; ii. 233, 307, 385, 459 *sq.* Literary
Associations, dislike to, ii. 293; his literary conservatism, ii. 470;
literary drudgery, attention to, i. 87; ii. 234; literary tastes,
when first called out, i. 471; his temperament, literary, ii. 186,
324. Literature, views regarding a life of, i. 93, 351; ii. 5, 38,
178, 437. Memory, his powers of, i. 28, 52, 53 and note, 54*n.*,
106, 136, 139, 185, 443; ii. 73, 198 *sq.*, 205, 206*n.*, 268, 284,
372, 390, 412, 458 *sq.*, 471*n.* Quotation, a growing habit of, i.
442; ii. 204. Wit and Humour, i. 76, 123, 128*n.*, 138 *sq.*, 186,
210, 230, 245, 250, 265, 338, 377 *sq.*, 381, 385 *sq.*, 404, 415,
429 *sq.*, 433; ii. 138, 145, 205, 374, 472, 475. *His Reading—*
early fondness for, i. 27, 56, 60 *sq.*, 68, 452; ii. 329, 464; his
love of, i. 134, 363, 369, 379, 396, 418, 439, 450; ii. 8, 18, 23,
204, 208, 244 *sq.*, 278, 392, 396, 431, 476, 478, 484. *Habits of
Reading*—aloud, ii. 273, 332; in bedroom, i. 54, 112; ii. 74,
233, 248, 264; before breakfast, i. 280, 437, 455; at breakfast,
ii. 22, 247, 476; Greek, i. 45, 436 *sq.*, 439; quick reading, i.
54; ii. 215, 247, 300 and note, 472; Sunday reading in 1835,
i. 456, 475; thirteen months' reading, i. 452; while travelling,
i. 325, 379; ii. 267-269, 418; while walking, i. 325; ii. 273,
292, 302, 331, 393*n.* (For his *Marginalia* see *List of Writings.*)
Particular subjects of reading :—ballad literature, ii. 96 and note;
calculations, calendars, etc., ii. 205, 436 *sq.*, 459 *sq.*; Chrysostom,
he strains at, i. 473; classics, "insatiable love" of the, i. 183,
444, 457; historians, i. 189, 475; ii. 241, 247, 249, 391; history,
English, i. 363; French, ii. 20; military operations, ii. 379;
novel-reading, i. 98 *sq.*, 136, 470; religious controversy, works
of, i. 63; ii. 219, 473; Queen Anne's time, the literature of, ii.
455; scholarship, points of, i. 120, 440; ii. 132, 431, 437. *His
Library*—foundation of, i. 35 *sq.*, 188, 419, 471; ii. 15*n.*, 266,
278; his first prize, i. 419; books for India, i. 361-363, 390 *sq.*,
452; ii. 74; at Clapham, ii. 297. *Certain dislikes*—bad poets, i.
128; law, i. 113, 447; mathematics, i. 45, 86, 90; new lights, ii.
469; poetry, modern English, i. 459; verse-making, Greek and

INDEX TO TREVELYAN'S LIFE OF MACAULAY. 51

MACAULAY (Lord), *continued*:—
Latin, i. 84; ii. 288, 381; the worst thing in Greek, i. 465; the worst thing in ancient Latin, i. 466. *Favourite Writers and Books*:— Æschylus, i. 437, 482; a valuable American book, ii. 329; Athenian writers, the six first-rate, ii. 433; Aulus Gellius, i. 458; Austen, Jane, i. 246; ii. 298, 477; Boswell's Johnson, i. 233, 419; Burke, ii. 385; Burnet, i. 339; Cæsar, i. 477; Cicero, i. 60, 91, 97, 450; ii. 395; Crabbe, ii. 426*n*.; Dante, i. 380; ii. 23, 202; Demosthenes, i. 449; ii. 431; Don Quixote, i. 339, 389; Maria Edgeworth, i. 246; ii. 238*n*.; Elizabethan drama, the highest form of composition, ii. 202; Euripides, i. 440, 482*n*.; favourites of his boyhood, i. 61, 134, 339, 419; ii. 9, 426*n*.; Gil Blas, ii. 46; Goethe, ii. 302*n*.; Grandison, i. 471; historians, ancient and modern, i. 439, 458; ii. 274, 289*n*.; Jeffrey, Francis, ii. 129; Latin, the most eloquent passages in, i. 466 *sq*.; the finest lines in, i. 379; lines, two favourite, ii. 22; Lessing, ii. 8; Milton, ii. 385; Molière, ii. 199; Paolo, Fra, ii. 289*n*.; Pickwick, i. 471; Plato, ii. 357*n*.; Poets, how ranked by him, i. 380, 437; ii. 202; Porson's Letters to Travis, ii. 40*n*., 293 and note; Prize-books for Schools, i. 418; Prayer-book, ii. 24; Robinson Crusoe, ii. 464; *Romans*, a passage in the Epistle to the, ii. 337*n*.; Schiller, his plays ranked, ii. 209; Shakespeare, his plays ranked, i. 380; ii. 202 *sq*., 307; Staël, Madame de, i. 246; Thucydides, i. 249, 449, 475; ii. 248, 392; women, three eminent, i. 246; writers, his taste for certain bad, i. 349*n*.; ii. 477; Xenophon, i. 475. (*See also separate headings.*)
v. HIS WORK AS A WRITER, AND A LIST OF HIS WRITINGS:—*Habits of work* :—carefulness, i. 341, 461; ii. 220-222, 230-232, 230*n*.; difficulties of working :—in setting to work, ii. 453 *sq*.; in working during a political crisis, ii. 341; on a number of subjects simultaneously, ii. 128, 164; against the grain, i. 113; ii. 230, 280; of making a tolerable book, ii. 385; energy and industry, i. 261, 330, 422; ii. 220-222, 222 and note, 228, 230, 244, 385, 389, 457; idleness, confessions of, i. 188, 261; ii. 321; method and times of working, ii. 227-229, 229*n*., 263, 271; at *British Museum*, ii. 400; the pleasure he took in his work, i. 461, 472. *His own opinion of his work* :—dissatisfied with his own productions, i. 233, 341; ii. 125, 233, 236, 263, 468; epitaph-writing, his attempt at, ii. 230*n*.; of his *Essays*, i. 461; ii. 109, 113 *sq*., 129, 131*n*., 260, 272; his favourite of his early writings, i. 119; fine arts and poetry, regrets his criticisms on, ii. 8; his forte in style and composition, ii. 107, 293; his hand not a light one, i. 338; of his

MACAULAY (Lord), *continued* :—

History, ii. 236, 241, 247 *sq.*, 273, 297, 398*n.*, 451 ; indifferent to others' opinion, i. 60, 337 ; literary success, cause of his, ii. 230, 280, 461; (*see* i. 360;) mistrusts his own judgment, i. 266 ; ii. 130; claimed not the title of poet, ii. 323 ; will not write on religious controversy, ii. 81; of one of his Valentines, ii. 297 ; his most careful work up till 1837, i. 461; his writings, a disagreeable subject to him, ii. 35, 259; thinks his writing improved to the last, ii. 457. *His Style* :—how thought of by Cambridge examiners, i. 86 ; accuracy, i. 55, 189; ii. 73, 131, 220 *sq.*, 243, 471*n.*; clearness, i. 186, 189 ; ii. 235, 277 ; forecasts, his fondness for, i. 268, 303 ; ii. 136, 202, 215, 250 *sq.*, 258, 277 ; Jeffrey's admiration of, i. 122.

LIST OF HIS WRITINGS :—The most popular, i. 371*n*. *a. Unpublished productions of his childhood*: Compendium of History, i. 30; on the Conversion of Travancore, i. 30; battle of Cheviot, i. 31; Olaus the Great, i. 31–33; Hymns, i. 31; Fingal, i. 32; Childe Hugh, i. 35 ; Verses to General Macaulay, i. 36 ; Roderic, i. 55 ; on Napoleon, i. 55 ; on the entry of the allies into Paris, i. 55 ; Don Fernando, i. 56; Poem on Babington, i. 56; Waterloo column, inscription for, i. 60.

b. Earliest Published Writings :—Index to the 13th vol. of *Christian Observer*, i. 62 ; letter on Novel-writing in 15th vol. of *Christian Observer*, i. 62.

c. Cambridge Prize Essays and Poems: English prize poems, i. 83, 93 ; Latin Declamation, i. 84 ; essay on William III., i. 86–88; poem on Waterloo, i. 94.

d. Knight's Quarterly Magazine:—ii. 123, 328 ; two poems, i. 117; paper on West Indian Slavery, i. 117; Roman story, i. 118 *sq.*; ii. 460; Athenian story, i. 119 ; on the Royal Society of Literature, i. 118 ; on Cowley and Milton, i. 119; St. Dennis and St. George, ii. 393*n.*; Ivry, ii. 448.

e. Edinburgh Review :—Macaulay well received in social circles in his character of an Edinburgh Reviewer, i. 181; his articles praised by S. Smith, i. 148 ; the invention of the kind of composition due to Southey, ii. 109 ; his first attempt at narrative, i. 255; on certain omissions made in one of the articles, i. 155 ; Napier's criticisms on *Frederic the Great*, ii. 108–110 ; scriptural allusions in *Mirabeau*, i. 274 ; his articles regulate the sale of *Review*, i. 304 ; might have all been written in Calcutta, i. 356 ; offers to write in India, i. 356 *sq.*; the most popular, i. 371*n.*; his own estimate of them, i. 461; ii. 109, 113 *sq.*, 129, 131*n.*,

MACAULAY (Lord), *continued :—*
260, 272 ; his favourite place in the *Review*, ii. 107 ; his articles cut out and bound up, ii. 112 ; rumour that he no longer wrote for, ii. 163. *The Subjects :*—Addison, i. 371*n.*, 427 ; ii. 128, 130, 131*n.*, 259 *sq.*, 263 ; d'Arblay, i. 184*n.*; ii. 111; Bacon, i. 220*n.*, 460–463, 471 *sq.*; ii. 36*n.*, 363*n.*; Barère, ii. 152-154; Boswell, i. 129, 233, 245, 251, 254, 255 and note, 356; ii. 146*n.*, 243, 457 ; Bunyan, i. 195 ; ii. 126 ; Burleigh, i. 196, 255, 264, 267 ; ii. 239*n.*; Byron, i. 221 and note, 228, 231, 233, 371*n.*; Chatham (*first article*), i. 262, 357, 359, 362, 371*n.*; ii. 19*n.*; (*second article*), ii. 156 ; Clive, i. 371*n.*, 372*n.*, 376, 471 *sq.*; ii. 24, 68 *sq.*, 78 *sq*, 85, 107 ; Frederic, ii. 100*n.*, 106-108, 110, 296 ; Gladstone, ii. 50 *sq.*, 54, 79, 105*n.*; Hallam, i. 140, 191 ; Hampden, i. 255; Hastings, i. 261, 371*n.*, 372*n.*; ii. 81, 84 *sq.*, 101-103, 105-107, 324, 462 ; Holland, Lord, ii. 86*n.*, 97 *sq.*, 116 *sq.*, 324 ; Hunt, Leigh, ii. 80-82, 84 ; Jewish Disabilities, i. 156 ; Machiavelli, i. 140; Mackintosh, i. 362, 390, 471 ; ii. 3-7; Mahon, i. 311, 262 ; Mill, three articles on, i. 140, 141*n.*, 143, 155, 191 ; Milton, i. 121 *sq.*; Mirabeau, i. 263, 266 *sq.*, 274 ; Montgomery, i. 129, 200 ; ii. 281, 365*n.*, 393 ; Ranke, i. 39 ; ii. 31*n.*, 79 ; Sadler, two articles on, i. 128 *sq.*, 258 ; Southey, i. 141 *sq.*, 155; Temple, i. 120, 471 *sq.*; ii. 16 ; Walpole, i. 262, 337, 340-342, 341*n.*, 346 *sq.*

f. Lays of Ancient Rome :—i. 120 ; ii. 18, 27, 30, 37, 51, 94, 97, 114 and note, 117-126, 287, 430, 448, 462.

g. History of England :—Possible origin of the idea of writing, i. 87 ; design of writing a, i. 450 ; ii. 13 *sq.*, 37; begins it, ii. 69*n.*, 73, 105 ; its intended scope, ii. 14, 94, 105, 107*n.*; method of work on, ii. 222 and note, 223-227, 264, 271, 274, 297, 307, 372, 385 ; his mind concentrated on it, ii. 448 ; its title, ii. 235 ; a MS. page of, i. 400, 454*n.*; suggestions as to an Index, ii. 234*n.*; publication of First Part, ii. 236, 247-250, 252, 282, 394 ; of Second Part, ii. 315, 391 *sq.*; begins the 5th vol., ii. 452, 454, 483 ; statistics of sale, ii. 397, 398 and note, 419, 448 ; a wager on the sale of, ii. 248 ; the cheque for £20,000, ii. 419 ; various translations of, ii. 398*n.*; particular passages in, i. 39 ; ii. 218, 220-222, 231 *sq.*, 264, 273, 281, 282*n.*, 283, 297, 307, 385 *sq.*, 390, 394, 453 ; his feelings about it, ii. 294, 321-323, 360, 372, 375, 386 *sq.*, 389, 391-393, 396, 398*n.*, 451, 449, 441-454, 456, 484 ; he wonders at its popularity in America, ii. 398*n.*; the *History* in the House of Correction, ii. 239 ; Mr. Crump's bribe, ii. 202 ; the hippopotamus as a rival, ii. 259 ; Hume's History, ii. 258 ;

MACAULAY (Lord), *continued :—*

an impromptu on, ii. 463; one mistake in, ii. 394; the natural son's request, ii. 461; the Queen and James II., ii. 279; a Scotch tourist's remark on, ii. 482; the battle of Worcester, ii. 303. *Various*, ii. 106 *sq.*, 114, 117, 128, 133, 163, 171, 172*n.*, 178, 184, 187, 189, 215, 234 *sq.*, 241, 244 *sq.*, 258, 264, 266, 272, 428, 456. *General criticisms on :*—his critics' respect for him, ii. 478; his silence respecting, ii. 461; contented with, ii. 265, 271, 395; called a historical painter, ii. 309; greatly pleased with American, ii. 398*n*. *Particular criticisms:*—Adolphus, ii. 257, 394; Miss Aikin, ii. 259; from America, ii. 240, 398*n.*; Lord Auckland, ii. 237; Bagehot, W., ii. 227; Buckle, H. T., ii. 228; a Brighton sermon, ii. 395; Lord Carlisle, ii. 197, 454*n.*; Conybeare, ii. 250; Croker, ii. 242, 257, 263; Edgeworth, Miss, ii. 238; Graham, Sir J., ii. 245; Guizot, ii. 197, 396; Lord Halifax, ii. 237; Holland, Sir H., ii. 394; Jeffrey, ii. 237; Kemble, ii. 451 *sq.*; Lingard, ii. 243; from Londonderry, ii. 395; Paget, ii. 463; Phillpotts, Bp., ii. 257 and note; *Press* criticisms, ii. 241, (about Procopius) 243, 253, 394, 451 *sq.*, 461, 463; from *Punch*, ii. 240; Quakers, ii. 253, 256 and note; Ranke, ii. 398; Scotch criticisms, ii. 398*n.*; Spottiswoode's office, a reader in, ii. 235; Stephen, Sir J., ii. 394; Thackeray, ii. 220; Wellington, Duke of, ii. 253; Dukinfield, Working-Men of, ii. 239 and note.

h. Encyclopædia Britannica, ii. 241, 259, 456 *sq.*

i. Various Writings :—Armada, The, i. 262; ii. 448; Queen Caroline, Ode to, i. 101; Indian Minutes, and Indian Civil Service Report, see *suprà*, *India*; lines written in 1847, ii. 191–193, 448; Macaronic Poem on circuit, i. 113; Malkin, Sir B., inscription on monument of, i. 472; Martyn, H., epitaph on, i. 38*n.*; *Parson's Journey to Cambridge*, i. 233; Plautus, translation from, ii. 287 and note; *Political Georgics*, i. 232; *Sortes Virgilianæ*, i. 233; Scutari column, inscription for, ii. 379*n.*, 380*n.*; *Tears of Sensibility*, i. 108; Trevelyan's Prize Poem, lines added to, ii. 434; Valentines, ii. 212 *sq.*, 259, 297; Voltaire, inscription for a picture of, i. 145.

k. Doggrel verses and effusions of the "Judicious Poet," i. 137 *sq.*, 187, 196, 217, 241*n.*, 265–270, 304, 306 *sq.*, 311; ii. 197*n.*, 209, 211 *sq.*, 219, 271, 422.

l. Subjects discussed for writing on :—Austen, Jane, a review of her novels, i. 363; a short life of, ii. 477; Burke's life and writings, ii. 155 and note; Burnet's Characters, edited by Bishop Jebb, i. 390; Capefigue's Napoleon, ii. 80; Cobbett, W., an

INDEX TO TREVELYAN'S LIFE OF MACAULAY. 55

MACAULAY (Lord), *continued:*—
article on, ii. 286*n.*, Lord Cornwallis, ii. 115; day-dreams, ii. 461; Dickens's *American Notes*, ii. 117, 121 *sq.*; Education question in 1839, ii. 68; an epitaph for T. Babington, ii. 230*n.*; France, state of parties in, i. 171, 201–205; a history of France, 1814–1830, i. 172; Gladstone's second work on Church and State, ii. 79, 81; Italy, romantic poetry of, i. 390; ii. 24; Lockhart's Life of Scott, ii. 7–9; Morbidities, an essay on his, ii. 321; More, Hannah, i. 471; *Paradise Lost*, translation of a passage from, into Greek, ii. 268; Richardson's novels, i. 196; Romilly's Life, ii. 115 *sq.*; Lord Shaftesbury, the author of the Habeas Corpus Act, i. 471; the Thames, a descriptive poem on, ii. 388; Trevor's William III., ii. 107; Tyler's Henry V., ii. 106 and note; the Vernon correspondence, ii. 107; Voltaire, i. 362.

m. *Marginalia in his books:*—i. 238*n.*, 453, 468 *sq.*; ii. 475; books containing them, i. 31*n.*, 238 and note, 454, 466 and note, 467*n.*, 469 *sq.*, 475–482; ii. 289*n.*, 369*n.*, 426*n.*, 473 *sq.*, 475.

vi. HIS SPEECHES AND CHARACTERISTICS AS A SPEAKER:—his own *dicta* on the subject, i. 105, 179, 187, 209, 244, 254, 317; ii. 74, 177, 190, 261 *sq.*, 344, 373, 442; an extemporaneous reply, i. 244; a Lysias-like speech, ii. 357*n.*; testimony of others, i. 69, 116, 163, 175–178, 187, 197 *sq.*, 209, 234 *sq.*, 244 *sq.*, 254, 300, 317, 346; ii. 67, 137, 141, 142*n.*, 143*n.*, 162, 179 *sq.*, 342 *sq.*; made a debater by mobs, i. 290; his action and manner, i. 244; ii. 141, 142 and note; publication of a selection of, ii. 372–374. *A list of his speeches:*—at Cambridge on George III., i. 83; at Freemasons' Tavern in 1824, i. 114. *In the House of Commons:*—maiden speech i., 163; first session, i. 165; 23 Nov., 1830, i. 174; 2 March, 1831, i. 175, 181, 187; 5 July, 1831, i. 198, 234; ii. 373; an extemporaneous speech, i. 244; 30 Sept., 1831, i. 198; 16 Dec., 1831, i. 198; 28 Feb., 1832, ii. 357*n.*; 6 Feb., 1833, i. 297 and note; 10 July, 1833, i. 300, 317, 327; ii. 179*n.*, 346*n.*, 373; 24 July, 1833, i. 314, 320 *sq.*; 18 June, 1839, ii. 65–67; tried to speak on *Education question*, ii. 68; first *Army Estimate*, ii. 73; 29 Jan. 1840, ii. 74; 7 April, 1840, ii. 75; *Irish Registration Bills*, speeches on, ii. 76–78; 5 Feb., 1841, ii. 136; 5 March, 1841, ii. 86; 6 April, 1842, ii. 136 and note; 9 March, 1843, i. 129; ii. 140, 373; 6 June, 1844, ii. 160, 374; 24 June, 1844, ii. 160; 14 April, 1845, ii. 161–163; 23 April, 1845, ii. 160; 9 July, 1845, ii. 160; speeches in 1846-7, ii. 179; 10 March, 1846, ii. 180; 22 May, 1846, ii. 179 and note; 1 June, 1853, ii.

INDEX TO TREVELYAN'S LIFE OF MACAULAY.

MACAULAY (Lord), *continued*:—
341-344; 24 June, 1853, ii. 348-356; 19 July, 1853, ii. 356-358;
in the House of Lords twice prepared to speak, ii. 442; Leeds
election of 1832, i. 288, 290 *sq.*; at Edinburgh in 1847, ii. 194*n.*;
in 1852, ii. 249*n.*, 283*n.*, 334, 337; at Glasgow in 1849, ii. 261 *sq.*
vii. REMARKS, OPINIONS, SENTIMENTS:—ancient events, the
best way of poetically treating, ii. 45; architecture, the sublime
in, ii. 147, 269; art and artists, criticisms on, i. 217, 219, 231,
242, 265; ii. 8, 21 *sq.*, 33, 41 *sq.*, 113, 210, 217, 230 *sq.*, 330 *sq.*,
363, 364*n.*, 416-418, 429, 430 and note, 465; authors, never hurt
by attacks, ii. 241, 243; gregarious authors, dislikes the notion
of, ii. 293; likes to give a sample of a favourite author's wares,
ii. 204; Bible as a model of English language, i. 214; Boards,
the utility of, ii. 248; *books*—the art of making a book amusing,
ii. 44*n.*; a book to be recommended must be amusing, ii. 278; on
foreign books, i. 389; every book settles its own place, ii. 121;
on prize-books, i. 419; canvassing at elections, on, i. 285 *sq.*; children the only true poets, ii. 207; Cold Bath Fields, a broken
head in, i. 301*n.*; Commons, House of, on success in, i. 179, 209;
competitive examinations, ii. 354 *sq.*; conversational powers, the
real use of, i. 243; death, thoughts on, i. 326 *sq.*, 480; ii. 278,
323, 362; on the deaths of friends, i. 327; ii. 291; despotism
and free government, i. 404; diaries, i. 272, 469; ii. 246*n.*, 396;
economical maxims, ii. 421; epitaph-writing, ii. 230*n.*; England,
the curse of, i. 338; ex-lions, ii. 251*n.*; fools, general combination
of, ii. 150; Ghibelline preferences, his, ii. 21; genius—vulgar
idea of, ii. 363; always takes its own course, ii. 467; a poor
plea for immorality, ii. 426*n.*; gentlemen, the world not made
only for, ii. 279; heraldry, i. 415; history, the "dignity of," ii.
110; on chronological order in writing, ii. 249; on acting
honourably and uprightly, i. 332; imagination, works of, i. 93;
index, on the subject of an, ii. 234*n.*; individuality of the age, ii.
467; independence of others, i. 378; life, fascination of, i. 326;
public life, i. 309, 450 *sq.*; languages, the growth of, i. 419;
literary history, ii. 464; logic and rhetoric, i. 416; memory, a
danger of a good, i. 443; Methodist and pedant, the terms, i.
100; oaths of Parliamentary Committees, ii. 47; olive-trees,
thoughts on, ii. 22, 43; periodical writings, i. 155 *sq.*; ii. 11, 112;
philosophers, natural, ii. 450; political economy, ii. 468; political prejudices, ii. 47; politics and literature, the paths of, compared, i. 451; printing and steam, discoveries of, ii. 202; racing,
ii. 185. *Religious Notes and Views*:—declaration at Leeds, i.

MACAULAY (Lord), continued :—
289; his views kept behind a veil, ii. 97; loyalty to the Church, ii. 409; no "love for establishments or for priests," ii. 358; how he regarded ecclesiastical matters, ii. 183; cares not to engage in theological controversy, ii. 81; religion and politics, the questions of in 1838, ii. 58; Papal endowment, ii. 248; Papal government, ii. 34 *sq.*; Anglo-Catholic cant, ii. 197*n.*, 290 *sq.*; his neutrality on the subject of propagating Christianity, ii. 446 *sq.*; on Middleton's *Free Inquiry*, ii. 473*n.*; on miracles, ii. 200, 473*n.*; the superstition of an oath, ii. 47; the doctrine of the Trinity, ii. 200; Bolingbroke, ii. 391; Gibbon, ii. 40*n.*; the Fathers, ii. 40*n.*, 474*n*; on the representative system in government. i. 286; on revolutions, ii. 443; scholar, his definition of a, i. 84; the term, i. 100; schools, on speechifying at, i. 417; separation from friends, ii. 405*n.*; slavery, i. 24*n.*; Seventh Day, on the observation of the, ii. 336*n.*; teaching, an advantage to the teacher from, i. 110; University honours, i. 89; ii. 346*n*, 352; versification, Greek and Latin, i. 84; ii. 288, 381; war, ii. 83; youthful distinction, ii. 346*n.*, 352 *sq.*, 381; woman's love measured by the eminence of men, i. 267; the world and gentlemen, ii. 279; writing, the first rule of all, ii. 110.

viii. LETTERS WRITTEN BY HIM TO :—Black, Adam, (July 14, 1841), ii. 185.

Ellis, T. F., (March 30, 1831), i. 206; (Oct. 17, 1831), i. 253; (July 1, 1834), i. 376; (Dec. 15, 1834), i. 435; (Feb. 8, 1835), i. 438; (May 29, 1835), i. 443; (Aug. 25, 1835), i. 447; (Dec. 30, 1835), i. 449; (May 30, 1836), i. 454; (July 25, 1836), i. 457; (Nov. 30, 1836), i. 465; (March 8, 1837), i. 468; (Dec. 18, 1837), i. 472; (Sep. 15, 1838), ii. 15; (July 12, 1841), ii. 94; (Aug. 22, 1842), ii. 118; (Sep. 29, 1842), ii. 120; (Feb. —, 1843), ii. 139; (no date), ii. 181; (July 30, 1847), ii. 191; (July 17, 1848), ii. 220; (July 27, 1848), ii. 221; (Sep. 3, 1850), ii. 285; (Sep. 8, 1850), ii. 285; (Aug. 21, 1851), ii. 300; (Sep. 12, 1851), ii. 301.

Hudson, Mr., of the East India House, (Aug. 22, 1815), i. 57.

Lansdowne, Marquis of, (Dec. 5, 1833), i. 350; (Feb. 15, 1834), i. 367.

Leeds Elector in 1832, a, (Aug. 3, 1832), i. 285.

Macaulay, Fanny, (Aug. 10, 1834), i. 381; (June 28, 1841), ii. 93; (June 19, 1852), ii. 314.

Macaulay, Hannah More (Lady Trevelyan), *written in* 1831, i. 209, 211, 212, 215, 217, 220, 222, 225, 227, 230, 232, 234, 235,

MACAULAY (Lord), *continued:*—
236, 239, 240, 241, 244, 246, 249, 252; *in* 1832, i. 262, 263, 265, 267, 268, 269, 271, 273, 275, 278, 279, 281, 283, 294, 295; *in* 1833, i. 301, 303, 305, 308, 310, 317, 318, 320, 321, 322, 324, 326, 327, 330, 336, 337, 339, 342, 344, 345, 348, 353, 357; (Jan. 2, 1834), i. 359; (Jan. 4, 1834), i. 361; (March 20, 1839), ii. 52; (Oct. 9, 1844), ii. 157; (Dec. 11, 1845), ii. 164; (Dec. 13, 1845), ii. 168; (Dec. 19, 1845), ii. 170; (Dec. 20, 1845), ii. 172; (July 30, 1847), ii. 191.

Macaulay, Margaret (Mrs. E. Cropper), *jointly with H. M. Macaulay*, i. 222, 262, 263, 265, 267, 268, 269, 271, 273, 275, 278; *to her alone*, (Dec. 7, 1834), i. 391.

Macaulay, Mrs. Zachary, his mother, (April 20, 1813), i. 42; (Aug. 14, 1813), i. 47; (April 11, 1814), i. 50; (Aug. 23, 1815), i. 58; (post-mark, 1818), i. 90; (March 25, 1821), i. 103; (July —, 1821), i. 105; (Nov. 2, 1821); i. 109; (April 15, 1828), i. 150.

Macaulay, Selina, *jointly with Fanny Macaulay*, (Aug. 10, 1834), i. 381.

Macaulay, Zachary, his father, (Feb. 22, 1813), i. 40; (April 26, 1813), i. 43; (May 8, 1813), i. 44; (Nov. 9, 1818), i. 91; (Feb. 5, 1819), i. 92; (September —, 1819), i. 96; (Jan. 5, 1820), i. 98; (Nov. 13, 1820), i. 102; (Aug. 31, 1821), i. 106; (July 26, 1822), i. 110; (Oct. 1, 1824), i. 110; (July 9, 1823), i. 118; (Oct. 7, 1824), i. 120; (April 2, 1826), i. 144; (July 21, 1826), i. 146; (July 26, 1826), i. 147; (Sep. 1, 1827), i. 148; (March 14, 1829), i. 154; (Feb. 10, 1830), i. 156; (Paris, September 26), i. 206; (July 22, 1833), i. 319; (Oct. 12, 1836), i. 463.

Napier, Macvey, (Jan. 25, 1830), i. 155; (March 22, 1830), i. 200; (Aug. 19, 1830), i. 200; (Sep. 16, 1830), i. 203; (Jan. 9, 1832), i. 255; (Jan. 19, 1832), i. 255; (Oct. 21, 1833), i. 341; (Dec. 5, 1833), i. 355; (Feb. 13, 1834), i. 362; (Dec. 10, 1834), i. 390; (Nov. 26, 1836). i. 460; (Nov. 28, 1836), i. 462; (June 15, 1837), i. 471; (June 14, 1838), ii. 5; (Aug. 14, 1838), ii. 6; (June 26, 1838), ii. 7; (July 20, 1838), ii. 10; (Nov. 4, 1838), ii. 24; (Feb. 26, 1839), ii. 51; (July 4, 1839), ii. 68; (Sep. 2, 1839), ii. 68; (Sep. 20, 1839), ii. 69; (November 1839), ii. 78; (Oct. 14, 1840), ii. 79; (Oct. 29, 1840), ii. 80; (Nov. 13, 1840), ii. 81; (Dec. 8, 1840), ii. 82; (Jan. 11, 1841), ii. 84; (April 26, 1841), ii. 85; (July 27, 1841), ii. 97; (Oct. 26, 1841), ii. 103; (Oct. 30, 1841), ii. 103; (Nov. 5, 1841), ii. 105; (Dec. 1, 1841), ii. 106; (April 18, 1842), ii. 108; (April 25, 1842), ii. 111; (June 24, 1842), ii. 112; (July 14, 1842), ii.

MACAULAY (Lord), continued :—
114; (July 20, 1842), ii. 116; (Oct. 19, 1842), ii. 121; (Nov. 16, 1842), ii. 124; (Dec. 3, 1842), ii. 125; (Jan. 18, 1843), ii. 127; (April 19, 1843), ii. 128; (June 15, 1843), ii. 130; (July 22, 1843), ii. 130; (Nov. 25, 1843), ii. 149; (Dec. 13, 1843), ii. 152; (April 10, 1844), ii. 153; (Aug. 14, 1844), ii. 155; (Jan. 4, 1846), ii. 175; (Jan. 10, 1846), ii. 176.
Secretary of the Scottish Reformation Society, (June 23, 1852), ii. 316.
Trevelyan, G. O., (Aug. 1, 1853), ii. 432.
Trevelyan, Margaret, (Sep. 15, 1842), ii. 207; (Oct. 14, 1851), ii. 209.
Whewell, Rev. Dr., (Oct. 9, 1857), ii. 436.

MACAULAY, Zachary, his birth, and work in Jamaica, i. 9 *sq.*; returns to England, i. 11; sails for Sierra Leone, i. 12; becomes Governor, i. 12; his position and duties, i. 12–15; his conduct during the invasion of Sierra Leone by French sailors, 15–21; his return home and introduction to Selina Mills, i. 21; goes out again to Sierra Leone, i. 22; finally leaves Africa, and marries, i. 25; appointed Secretary of the Sierra Leone Company, i. 25; moves to Clapham, i. 27; goes into business as an African merchant, i. 37; pecuniary troubles, i. 129; his character and occupations, i. 44, 61 *sq.*, 65 *sq.*, 132; ii. 2; his friendships, i. 66 *sq.*, 316, 370; ii. 2, 12, 311*n.*; Buxton's estimate of his work, i. 317; described in *Edinburgh Review*, i. 70*n.*; Gladstone's mention of in Parliament, ii. 89; relations with his son when a child, i. 28, 33, 38, 60 *sq.*; his Toryism, i. 96; his sympathy with Queen Caroline, i. 100; suit against *John Bull* newspaper, i. 114; at a meeting of the Anti-Slavery Society at Freemasons' Tavern in 1824, i. 116; his dislike to *Knight's Quarterly Magazine*, i. 117; moves to Cadogan Place, i. 129; to great Ormond Street, i. 130; no real sympathy between father and son, i. 139; Macaulay's feeling towards his father, i. 67 *sq.*; their action respecting the West India Bill, i. 314; urges his son to speak on Wilberforce's death in Parliament, i. 329; applies to him about P——, i. 338, 343; about Lushington, i. 345; failing health and death, ii. 2 *sq.*; his *letters* to his son, i. 44, 48, 140, 395, 463.

MACCULLOCH, Mr., his wager on the sale of Macaulay's *History*, ii. 248.
MACDONALD, Sir James, i. 210, 243; his death from cholera, i. 264.
MACFARLAN, J. F., Macaulay's letter to him in 1846, ii. 173–176.
MACHIAVELLI, i. 217, ii. 23; how Macaulay ranked him among Italian historians, i. 458. See *Macaulay—Writings*.

MACKENZIE, Henry, his *Lounger*, and *Mirror*, i. 61.
MACKENZIE, Right Hon. Holt, his praise of the Indian Penal Code, ii. 44.
MACKENZIE, J. A. Stewart, M.P. for Ross-shire, i. 302, 333.
MACKINTOSH, Right Hon. Sir James, his regard for Z. Macaulay, i. 66; his commendation of Macaulay's maiden speech in Parliament, i. 163; gives Macaulay a letter of introduction to La Fayette, i. 169; was not a success in Parliament, i. 179; his feeling towards Brougham, i. 193; his praise of one of Macaulay's Reform speeches, i. 198; his kindness to Macaulay when young, i. 229n; Lardner's treatment of, 351; Macaulay differs from on the subject of Bacon's philosophy, i. 460; his *History of the Revolution*, edited by Wallace ii. 3-7; his powers not concentrated on any great work, ii. 128, 163; *alluded to*, i. 228, 229n., 274; ii. 124.
M'LAREN, Lord Provost, candidate for Edinburgh at the election of 1852, ii. 319.
MACLEOD, Sir John M., on the Indian Law Commission with Macaulay, i. 122n., 421 *sq.*, 431; ii. 236, 262.
MACNAGHTEN, Sir W., i. 431; at Ootacamund with Macaulay, i. 386; ii. 159.
MACNEILE, Rev. Hugh (afterwards Dean of Ripon), ii. 150.
MACROBIUS, i. 469.
MAGEE, William (Archbishop of Dublin), i. 271.
Magnetoscope, the, ii. 309.
MAHON, Lady, ii. 414.
MAHON, Lord (5th Earl Stanhope), a great friend of Macaulay's, i. 213, 239, 249; ii. 318; his Copyright Bill, ii. 136; tries to defend Clarendon against Hallam and Macaulay, ii. 198; defeated at Hertford Election in 1852, ii. 318; entertains Macaulay at Chevening, ii. 413; *alluded to*, i. 213, 239, 249, 273n., 434n.; ii. 53n., 196, 199, 243, 253, 306 *sq.*, 309 *sq.*, 316, 465, 489.
MAIDSTONE, Lord, M.P. for North Northants in 1837, his conduct in the House of Commons on an Irish night, ii. 77; *alluded to*, ii. 330, 335.
MAINE, Duc du, mention of in Macaulay's *History*, ii. 462n.
MAITLAND, ——, in connection with the Edinburgh Annuity Tax Bill, in 1853, ii. 357.
MALDEN, Henry, Professor of Greek at University College, London, at school with Macaulay, i. 40, 52, 56, 60; at Cambridge with him, i. 82, 84, 99, 111; ii. 410n.
MALKIN, Sir Benjamin Heath, a college friend of Macaulay, i. 90; his character, i. 342 *sq.*; a Judge in Calcutta, i. 342n., 438; his death, i. 472 and note; *alluded to*, i. 419, 431, 442.

MALKIN, Lady, i. 472.
MALTHUS, Rev. T. R., attacked by Sadler, i. 128; pleased with Macaulay's answers to Sadler, i. 128n.
Malvern, Macaulay at, ii. 214, 300-304.
Manchester, Reform meeting held in 1819 at, i. 95-97; its population in 1685, ii. 220 sq.
MANGLES, R. D., a friend of Macaulay in Calcutta, i. 431.
MANSFIELD and BABINGTON, firm of, i. 280.
MANSFIELD, Lord, Chief Justice of England, i. 342; ii. 258, 277, 381.
MANSFIELD, 3rd Earl of, i. 210.
MANZONI's *Promessi Sposi*, ii. 418.
Marble quarries in ancient times, ii. 32 sq.
Marginalia in Macaulay's books. See *Macaulay—Writings*.
MARKHAM's *New Children's Friend*, i. 418.
MARKLAND, Jeremiah, his correction of a corrupt passage in Euripides, i. 256.
MARMONTEL's *Memoirs*, i. 362, 415; ii. 100n.
MARRYAT, Captain, ii. 117.
MARSH, Dr. Herbert (successively Bishop of Llandaff and of Peterborough), i. 50 sq.
MARSHALL, John, M.P. for Leeds in 1832, i. 258, 288, 294.
MARSHALL, Mr., a former M.P. for Yorkshire, i. 211, 222.
MARSHALL, W., M.P. for Beverley, i. 249.
MARTIAL, i. 54, 446; Macaulay's opinion of, ii. 459.
MARTIN, John, painter, i. 227.
MARTIN, Sir Ranald, ii. 485 and note, 486.
MARTINEAU, Harriet, ii. 117; *quoted* on the subject of Copyright, ii. 134.
Martinus Scriblerus, ii. 455.
Martyrs, Book of, Fox's, the copy in the English College at Rome, ii. 32; the copy in Cheddar Church, ii. 324, 327; the copy in Wrington Church, ii. 328.
Masks and Faces, Mrs. Stirling's acting in, ii. 214.
Masterton, Henry, a novel, i. 266.
MATHEWS, Charles, *Life of*, ii. 294.
MATTHIÆ's correction of a corrupt passage in *Euripides*, i. 256.
MAULE, Fox (Lord Panmure), ii. 305; asks Macaulay to write inscription for Scutari column, ii. 379n.
MAULE, Sir William (Mr. Justice), his *dictum* about schools, i. 39.
MAUPERTUIS, P. L. Moreau de, French mathematician, ii. 107.
MAXWELL. See *Stirling-Maxwell*.
"May, our ten days of," i. 291.

MAY, Sir Erskine, his *Parliamentary Practice* quoted, i. 207n.
MAYNOOTH College, Macaulay's speeches in 1845 on the grant to, ii. 161 and note; the ground of opposition to his re-election for Edinburgh in 1846, ii. 178; and in 1847, ii. 182; his views on the subject inquired about in 1852, ii. 316; *alluded to*, i. 271; ii. 177 *sq*.
MAZARIN, Cardinal, Talleyrand's remark about, i. 237.
MAZZINI, Joseph, affair of his letters, and Sir J. Graham, ii. 160.
MEDICI, Cosmo de', ii. 42.
MEDICI, Lorenzo de', a model of Michael Angelo's statue of, i. 231; ii. 22.
MEEKE, Mrs., Novel-writer, Macaulay's intimate acquaintance with her works, i. 136, 296, 349 and note.
MELBOURNE, Viscount, Prime Minister, urges Macaulay to become Judge-Advocate, ii. 27; offers the Secretaryship-at-War in 1839, ii. 69; his Administration, decline and fall of, ii. 55–63, 82; Macaulay's remark about the great error of his government, ii. 166; his series of Royal Commissions, ii. 60.
MELVILL, Rev. H., one of the Indian Civil Service Committee of 1854, ii. 380n.
MELVILLE, Viscount. See *Dundas*.
MERIVALE, the family of, ii. 202.
MERLE D'AUBIGNÉ, J. H., Macaulay gives Queen Victoria his opinion of his *History of the Reformation*, ii. 295.
Metaurus, battle of the, Macaulay's remarks on the, i. 479 *sq*.
METCALFE, Sir Charles (Lord), Macaulay's high opinion of, ii. 352.
Methodist, name of, i. 100; preacher at Leeds election of 1832, i. 288; members of that persuasion at Sierra Leone, i. 23.
METTERNICH, Prince von, Talleyrand's remark about, i. 237.
MICHAEL ANGELO, i. 231.
MIDDLETON, Conyers, D.D., his *Free Enquiry*, ii. 197n., 473, 474n.; his *Letters*, ii. 473; his *Life of Cicero*, i. 418; Macaulay's opinion of, ii. 473n.
MIGUEL, Don, usurper to the throne of Portugal in 1828, i. 303.
MILL, ———, a son of James, Macaulay meets in India, i. 464.
MILL, James, Macaulay's attacks on his creed, i. 140 *sq*., 141n., 191; recommends Macaulay for the Indian appointment, i. 344; Macaulay meets and likes him, i. 358; his *History of India*, i. 379; ii. 85; his death a grief to Macaulay, i. 464.
MILL, John Stuart, his testimony to Macaulay's attacks upon his father's creed, i. 141; *quoted* for estimate of Macaulay as a young man, i. 79; his book on *Liberty*, ii. 467; *alluded to*, i. 191, 254.

INDEX TO TREVELYAN'S LIFE OF MACAULAY. 63

MILLER, Hugh, *quoted* for remark on the Edinburgh election of 1847, ii. 189.

MILLETT, F., one of the Indian Law Commission in 1835, i. 422.

MILLS, Mr., Macaulay's grandfather, i. 21.

MILLS, Mr., son of preceding, i. 21.

MILMAN, H. H., Dean of St. Paul's, Macaulay delighted by his appointment to St. Paul's, ii. 273; tells Macaulay about Holly Lodge, ii. 403; his Latin Christianity, ii. 403 and note; *quoted* for criticism on Milner's *History of the Church*, ii. 289n.; *alluded to*, ii. 53n., 168, 199, 202, 253, 256, 310, 489.

MILNER, Isaac, Dean of Carlisle, President of Queen's College, Cambridge, his kindness to Macaulay as a boy, i. 40, 42, 51.

MILNER, Joseph, his *History of the Church*, Macaulay's view of, ii. 289 and note; Milman's criticism on, ii. 289n.

MILNES, R. Monckton (Lord Houghton), on Macaulay's enjoyment of life, ii. 363; *alluded to*, ii. 198, 307, 437, 444.

MILTON, John, Macaulay's political opinions learnt from, i. 97; how ranked by him among the poets, i. 380, 437; ii. 202 *sq.*; compared with Æschylus, ii. 432; Macaulay knew *Paradise Lost* by heart, i. 53 and note, 106; ii. 268; his *Writings*, i. 267, 418; ii. 110, 137n., 138n., 203; *quoted*, i. 91, 283, 469, 482; ii. 268; *alluded to*, i. 99, 446; ii. 193, 385.

MILTON, Lord, M.P. (5th Earl Fitzwilliam), i. 241, 259; ii. 439. See *Fitzwilliam, 5th Earl*.

Minerva Press, The, i. 466.

MINTO, 2nd Earl of, ii. 139.

Miseries of Human Life, The, ii. 145.

MOHUN, Lord, his duel with the Duke of Hamilton in 1712, ii. 116.

MOLESWORTH, Sir William, Secretary of State for the Colonies, ii. 83.

MOLIÈRE, i. 85; ii. 148; Macaulay's favourite play of, ii. 199.

MOLTKE, Count von, Knight of the Prussian Order of Merit, ii. 399n.

MOLYNEUX, Misses, i. 264.

MONCRIEFF, James (Lord Moncrieff), ii. 337.

MONK, Dr., Bishop of Gloucester, Macaulay's Trinity Tutor, i. 138; ii. 329; his *Life of Bentley*, ii. 244n.

Monkeys, Physiology of, ii. 100n.

Monomotapa, A.D. 4551, a forecast, ii. 215.

MONSTRELET's *Chronicle*, i. 391.

MONTAGU, Basil, editor of Bacon's works, i. 220 and note, 226.

MONTAGUE, Charles, Chancellor of the Exchequer under William III., ii. 352, 375, 441.

MONTALEMBERT, Comte de, visit to Macaulay in 1858, ii. 443.
MONTGOMERY, Robert, Macaulay proposes to review his poetry, i. 200; writes to beg Macaulay to withdraw his review from his collected Essays, ii. 280 *sq.*, 365 and note; his death, ii. 393; *alluded to*, i. 129; ii. 258.
MONTROSE, Marquis of, ii. 362; Ward's picture of his execution, ii. 430.
MOORE, Thomas, meets Macaulay at Rogers's, i. 231; again, i. 232; discussion about Macaulay's squibs in the *Times*, i. 232 *sq.*; meets him at dinner at Rogers's, i. 347; his *Life of Byron*, ii. 266 *sq.*, 455; *alluded to*, i. 222, 359, 418; ii. 472.
MOORE, Edward, his *Fables for the Female Sex*, i. 361.
MORE, Hannah, Zachary Macaulay's introduction to, i. 21; favours his suit to Selina Mills, i. 22; her anecdote of Macaulay and the old spirits, i. 28; her criticisms on his early hymns, i. 32; Macaulay's visits to at Barley Wood, i. 34–36, 35*n.*; lays the foundation of his library, i. 35, 471; her remark on Garrick's face, i. 151; left Macaulay by will her library, i. 188 and note; Dr. Johnson's opinion of, i. 233 and note; Macaulay unwilling to review her Life or Works, i. 471; her description of the Vicar of Cheddar, ii. 325, 327; her grave at Cheddar, ii. 329; Macaulay re-visits Barley Wood, ii. 329; mention of, ii. 390.
MORE, Patty, i. 22.
MORE, Sally, a novel by, ii. 368.
MORGAN, Lady (Sydney Owenson), i. 270, 325.
MORIER, James, author of *Hadji Baba*, i. 228.
MORLEY, Lady, ii. 415*n*.
MORPETH, Lord. See *Carlisle*.
MORRISON, Baillie, ii. 357.
MOSCHUS, i. 470.
MOTLEY, J. Lothrop, his visit to Macaulay, i. 24*n.*; agrees with him on the subject of slavery, i. 24*n.*
MOULTRIE, Rev. John, college friend of Macaulay, i. 78, 83–117; his *Dream of Life*, i. 78; *quoted*, i. 79, 124, 126; his lines on the death of Macaulay's sister, i. 396*n.*; his death, i. 78*n.*
MUDIE, Robert, *The Sea*, by, i. 418.
MULGRAVE, 2nd Baron, ii. 67.
MÜLLER's *History of Switzerland*, i. 473.
MUNDEN, Joseph, actor, ii. 294.
MURCHISON, Sir Roderick, meets Macaulay at breakfast, ii. 200.
MURE, Colonel, breakfasted with Macaulay, ii. 198.

MURRAY, John, his wish to have Macaulay on the staff of the *Quarterly Review*, i. 121; *alluded to*, i. 254, 390.
MURRAY, Lieut.-Gen. Sir George, G.C.B., M.P., Colonial Secretary in 1830; the Duke of Wellington's advice to, about speaking in Parliament, ii. 202.
Musæ Cantabrigienses, ii. 352.
Mysterious Mother, The, i. 342.

NAPIER, Colonel (Sir W. F. P.), Macaulay's admiration of as a military historian, i. 458.
NAPIER, Macvey, Editor of *Edinburgh Review*, Macaulay writes to him about the Sadler controversy, i. 128 and note; rescinds an arrangement about a proposed article of Macaulay, i. 171; his notice in the *Edinburgh* about a speech of Brougham's, i. 202; answers Macaulay's remonstrance, i. 205; praises Macaulay's article on Dumont, i. 267; his statement about the sale of the *Review*, i. 304; praises the article on Walpole, i. 340; Macaulay gives a bad account of, ii. 15; Brougham's behaviour to, ii. 15; Macaulay's request to, about the *Review*, ii. 121; succeeded as Editor by Empson, ii. 362*n*.; *alluded to*, i. 221, 262, 305; ii. 16, 197*n*.
NAPLES, King of, Ferdinand II., ii. 46, 254. See *Italy*.
NAPOLEON I. See *Buonaparte*.
NAPOLEON III., Macaulay's views of his government in 1858, ii. 443.
NASH, John, architect, ii. 416.
NATHAN, J., his *Reminiscences of Byron*, ii. 395.
NEPAUL, King of, i. 470 and note.
NERO, C. Claudius, his generalship at the battle of the Metaurus discussed, i. 479 *sq*.
New Holland, i. 380.
New Monthly Magazine, Bulwer appointed editor of, i. 246; he retires from, i. 329, 331; Macaulay puffed and abused in the number for August, 1833, i. 329.
New Zealanders, ii. 31.
Newark, M. T. Sadler's connection with, i. 258.
NEWCASTLE, 1st Duke of, ii. 19 and note.
NEWCASTLE, 4th Duke of, i. 258.
NEWDIGATE, Sir Roger, his prize at Oxford, i. 84.
NEWELL ——, captain of a Yankee Slaver, and Z. Macaulay, i. 16.
NEWMAN, John Henry (Cardinal), Macaulay's remark about certain of his writings, ii. 197*n*.; his *Lives of the Saints*, ii. 196; his *Lectures*, ii. 290; *alluded to*, ii. 209, 418.
NEWPORT, Sir John, M.P. for Waterford, i. 242.

Newspapers:—Age, ii. 412; Courier, ii. 113; Economist, ii. 227; Examiner, i. 82; ii. 113; Globe, ii. 113; John Bull, i. 101; Leader, ii. 341–343; Literary Gazette, ii. 232; Morning Chronicle, i. 82; ii. 24, 34, 266; Morning Herald, ii. 286*n.*; Morning Post, i. 108 *sq.*; ii. 61, 133, 266; Punch, ii. 241; Scotsman, ii. 174, 243, 318; Spectator, i. 405; Standard, ii. 113; Times, i. 232; ii. 24, 34, 70, 72, 113, 214*n.*, 243; a Cambridge county paper, i. 75; old newspapers at the British Museum, ii. 264.

NEWTON, Sir Isaac, i. 197, 457.

NEWTON, John, Slave Trader and Divine, founder of the Evangelical school, i. 9, 244; ii. 302.

NICHOLLS, Mr., mentioned in one of Macaulay's Indian Minutes, i. 413.

NICHOLS's *Literary Anecdotes*, ii. 426*n.*; Macaulay's annotation of, ii. 484.

NIEBUHR, B. G., Macaulay's view of his theory about Rome, i. 201, 445–447; ii. 114; his *History of Rome*, i. 461.

NIGGENS's *Earth*, i. 418.

NINON DE L'ENCLOS, Hannah More compared to, i. 471.

No-Popery, Macaulay's remark on the cry in 1850, ii. 200 and note; riots of 1780, i. 162, 302.

NOEL, Rev. Baptist, Minister of St. John's Chapel, Bedford Row, i. 132; his *Life of Bishop Wilson*, i. 224.

NORFOLK, Duchess of, Macaulay meets at Windsor Castle in 1850, ii. 295.

NORREYS, Lord, M.P. for Oxon, his behaviour in the House of Commons on an Irish night, ii. 77.

NORRIS, Henry, "Little Dicky," ii. 132.

North American Review. See *America.*

NORTH, Lord, Prime Minister 1770, compared with Lord Althorp, i. 248; *alluded to*, i. 302, 451; ii. 339.

NORTHCOTE, Sir Stafford, M.P., his Report on Civil Service Reform, ii. 383.

NORTHUMBERLAND, Dudley, Duke of, ii. 439.

NORTHUMBERLAND, 4th Duke of, i. 332; ii. 38.

NORTON, Hon. Mrs., the writer of the epitaphs on the dogs' gravestones at Oatlands, ii. 415*n.*

Nursery Rhymes, *quoted*, i. 395; ii. 119.

O'BRIEN, Stafford, ii. 199.

O'CONNELL, Daniel, M.P., compliments Macaulay on one of his Reform speeches, i. 234; his opposition to the address in Feb., 1833, i. 297; praises Macaulay's speech on the India Bill, i. 317; speaks

O'CONNELL, Daniel (*continued*):—
on the Sheil affair in 1834, i. 364 *sq.*; his charge against Election Committees in 1838, ii. 47; scene between him and Lord Maidstone in the House, ii. 78; *alluded to*, i. 271, 300 *sq.*, 433; ii. 133; "the O'Connell of Calcutta," i. 459.
O'CONNOR DON, The, M.P. for Roscommon in 1833, i. 304.
Oatlands, the Duchess of York's dog cemetery at, ii. 414*n.*, 415*n.*
Occult Sciences, Macaulay and his friends occupied with the, ii. 309.
ONSLOW, Arthur, Speaker 1728-1761, ii. 276, 368.
Orators, conversation on ancient, ii. 198.
OSSORY, Earl of, his duel with Villiers, 2nd Duke of Buckingham, ii. 115.
OVERSTONE, Lord, ii. 201.
OVID, i. 448, 477–479; *quoted*, i. 448; ii. 198.
OWEN, Professor Richard, ii. 449, 450 and note.
OWEN, Robert, Philanthropist, i. 226.
Oxford, Macaulay visits in 1831, i. 184 and note; drives through, i. 283 *sq.*; one of his favourite cities, ii. 21; working in the College Libraries at, ii. 222*n.*; made D.C.L. in 1856, ii. 399; the Observatory at, ii. 110; Wellington at, ii. 202; a bad school for medical education, ii. 295.

P——, Z. Macaulay's application to his son about, i. 338, 343.
PAGANINI, Nicolo, the violinist, i. 211.
PALEY, G. B., on a college reading-party with Macaulay, i. 105.
PALMER, Messrs., Bankers, i. 265.
PALMERSTON, Lord, Macaulay's favourite English statesman, ii. 254; praises a speech of Macaulay's, i. 317; Macaulay suggests his writing for the *Edin. Rev.*, ii. 118; difference between Lord Grey and him, ii. 171-173 *sq.*; his speech in Feb. 1849, ii. 254 and note; loses the Foreign Office, ii. 304; Macaulay's remark to Thiers about him, ii. 307; aids the Conservatives in 1852, ii. 312; his conduct in the matter of the Reform Banquet in 1854, ii. 377 *sq.*; a Harrow compliment to him, ii. 434 and note; universal approval of his making Macaulay a peer, ii. 435; *alluded to*, i. 248, 273, 276, 304; ii. 83, 133, 168, 367, 441.
PANIZZI, (Sir) Antonio, his edition of Boiardo, i. 390; his appointment as Principal Librarian at the British Museum, ii. 449 *sq.*; *alluded to*, ii. 198.
PAOLO, Fra (Sarpi), ranked by Macaulay at the head of Italian historians, i. 458; his favourite modern historian, ii. 289*n.*; *alluded to*, i. 380, 391; ii. 36, 274, 285-287, 460.
Papal Government, Macaulay's impressions of, in 1838, ii. 34 *sq.*, 41.

INDEX TO TREVELYAN'S LIFE OF MACAULAY.

Paris, Macaulay's impressions of, in 1830, i. 168-171, 189; *alluded to*, ii. 217, 436; his estimate of the Republicans of, in 1848, ii. 197.

PARK, Mungo, his *Travels*, i. 418.

PARKE, Baron (Lord Wensleydale), Macaulay meets him at Sydney Smith's in 1826, i. 147; Brougham and Macaulay dine with, in 1849, ii. 260; at a gathering of old Trinity Fellows, ii. 410*n*.; Macaulay dines with, ii. 299.

PARKER, Sir James, Vice-Chancellor, his death, ii. 323.

PARLIAMENT, on speaking in, i. 247; Wellington's advice about speaking in, ii. 202; a hard-worked, i. 183; first session of the Reformed, i. 297; dearth of talent in, in 1838, ii. 38; the Painted Chamber, i. 310; ii. 115. *House of Lords*: Macaulay's poor opinion of, i. 308 *sq.*, 449; his forecast of its fate, i. 305, 310; ii. 58; its influence during the last days of the Melbourne Ministry, ii. 56 *sq.*; Macaulay's scheme for its reconstruction, ii. 59; Irish Tithe Bill mutilated in, i. 450*n.*; Jewish Disabilities Bill thrown out in, i. 329; Corn Law Bill passed in 1846, ii. 177; Committee on Life Peerages, ii. 441*n.*; Macaulay takes his seat in, ii. 441; ready for speaking in, ii. 442. *House of Commons*: characteristics of life in, i. 178, 277, 330; Macaulay's zest for its life, i. 178; his station in, in 1831, i. 254; his remarks on success in, i. 179, 209; scenes in, 23 Nov., 1830, i. 174; 1 March, 1831, ii. 375; 22 March, 1831, i. 207-209; 11 July, 1831, i. 239; 15 Aug., 1832, i. 275-277; 29 Jan., 1833, i. 297; 11 June, 1840, ii. 77 *sq.*; opening night in 1849, ii. 254; in Nov., 1852, ii. 338; Budget night, Dec., 1852, i. 178; ii. 338; Education question, ii. 68, 150 and note; proved by Macaulay to be "The Beast of Revelation," i. 378; Macaulay's suggestion about portraits of great men for the new, ii. 33; the Reporters' Gallery, ii. 141-143; the Sheil affair, i. 364-366; the Smoking-room, i. 244, 269-271, 273*n.*, 304; the Ventilator, i. 276; *alluded to*, i. 218, 254, 276, 330, 442; ii. 55, 375. *Bills*: Ballot, in 1839, ii. 65; Bankruptcy Court, i. 180; Copyright, of 1842, ii. 134-138; Corn-Laws, ii. 88 *sq.*, 177; Duncombe's motion about the Chartists in 1842, ii. 183; Franchise, of 1866, i. 178; India, see *India*; Irish Church, i. 298, 308, 319, 326, 470; Registration of Voters in Ireland, ii. 76; Jewish Disabilities, i. 163, 329; Judges Exclusion, ii. 341-345; Maynooth College, ii. 161, 182, 316; Militia Bill, ii. 312, 335 and note; Negro Emancipation, i. 312-326; Orangemen's Processions, i. 275; Reform, of 1831-2, i. 165, 175, 183, 188, 213, 230, 252, 254, 258, 260; ii. 375; of 1852, ii. 305; of 1854, ii. 375; Scotch Church (Edinburgh Annuity Tax), ii. 356-358; Sugar Duties, ii. 89; see also *Macaulay—Speeches. Reform.*

INDEX TO TREVELYAN'S LIFE OF MACAULAY. 69

Parliamentary boroughs, Commissioners for arranging the boundaries of, in 1831, ii. 253 and note.
PARNELL, Thomas, *quoted*, i. 57.
PARR, Dr. Samuel, Macaulay's estimate of, ii. 264 ; story of him and Bentley, ii. 429.
PARSONS, R., the Jesuit, and the *Book of Martyrs*, ii. 32.
PASCAL, Blaise, his *Lettres Provinciales*, ii. 471 and note ; *quoted*, i. 255 ; *alluded to*, i. 185, 445 ; ii. 113, 199, 419.
PASQUIN, Tony, and Warren Hastings, ii. 84.
PASTA, Madame, i. 211, 215.
Patagonians in London, a forecast, ii. 31.
PEACOCK, Sir Barnes, his connection with Macaulay's Indian Penal Code, i. 426.
PEACOCK, G., Dean of Ely, ii. 304n.
PEACOCK, T. L., author of *Headlong Hall*, ii. 304 and note.
PEDRO, Don, and Portuguese affairs in 1832-3, i. 268, 303.
PEEL, Sir Robert, M.P., Prime Minister in 1834, i. 443n. ; ii. 55 *sq.* ; in opposition in 1838, ii. 59 ; his defence touching the Catholic question, ii. 465 *sq.* ; in the House of Commons, i. 179, 208, 267, 269, 297, 304 ; ii. 91, 162 ; praises Macaulay's Parliamentary speaking, i. 177, 197, 245, 300 ; ii. 67, 137 ; his character discussed by Lady Clanricarde, i. 237 ; Guizot's estimate of, ii. 466n. ; Macaulay meets him, ii. 276, 282 and note ; his death, ii. 283 ; *alluded to*, i. 253, 259, 329, 444, 470 ; ii. 167, 352, 431.
Peelites in the Aberdeen Ministry in 1852, ii. 341.
PENN, William, Lord W. Bentinck likened to, ii. 79 ; the Quakers' remonstrance with Macaulay about, ii. 253n., 256 ; Macaulay's opinion on the question unchanged, ii. 256 and note.
PEPYS, Samuel, his *Diary*, i. 134, 189 ; ii. 296, 431 ; Macaulay's dream about, ii. 428 ; *alluded to*, ii. 247, 268.
PERCEVAL, Spencer, Prime Minister in 1809, i. 70n., 187.
PERCY, Hugh, successively Bishop of Rochester, and Carlisle, i. 138.
PERCY, Thomas, Bishop of Dromore, his *Reliques* quoted, i. 59.
PERIZONIUS, his theory about early Roman history, ii. 114.
Persian war in 1857, and Lord Palmerston, ii. 434n.
PERSIUS, ii. 248.
PETER PINDAR (Dr. Wolcott), ii. 277.
PETER PRIM, Macaulay's servant in India, i. 372.
PETER THE GREAT, his statue at St. Petersburg, ii. 269.
Peterloo Massacre in 1819, the, i. 95-97, 260.
PETRARCH, i. 379 ; fate of his legacy of books to Venice, ii. 417.
PEYRONNET, M. de, Minister of Charles X., popular feeling against, in 1830, i. 170.

PHÆDRUS, i. 456.
PHILIP, Roman Emperor, A.D. 244, ii. 268.
PHILIPS, G. R., M.P. for Steyning, i. 216.
PHILIPS, Sir George, i. 216, 228, 280.
PHILLIPS, Thomas, R.A., ii. 53n.
PHILPOTTS, H., Bishop of Exeter, ii. 150; Macaulay's correspondence with, on certain statements in the *History* about the Church of England, ii. 256, 257 and note.
PHILO JUDÆUS, ii. 471.
PHOTIUS, a club rumour about Macaulay's reading, ii. 393 and note; ii. 394.
PICKERSGILL, F. R., portrait-painter, i. 268.
PINNOCK's editions of Goldsmith's *Histories*, i. 417.
PIOZZI, Mrs., and Hogarth's picture, the *Lady's Last Stake*, ii. 430n.
Pitt Diamond, the, i. 462.
PITT, William, Prime Minister, Sir P. Francis's remark about, i. 193; his contempt for Lord Sidmouth, ii. 276; Sir J. Sinclair's letter to, ii. 201; his action on the Slavery question in 1787 and 1799, i. 71; his statue in Hanover Square, ii. 213; his Tragedy written in 1772, ii. 413; story of Wilberforce and Fox touching him, i. 194; *alluded to*, i. 19, 69, 82, 159, 165, 239, 265, 316, 342; ii. 67, 91 *sq*.
PLATO, one of Macaulay's six first-rate Athenians, ii. 433; his vein of ridicule, i. 445; a ballad about, ii. 96; *alluded to*, i. 448, 452, ii. 248, 357n., 368–371, 419.
PLAUTUS, i. 452 *sq*., 475; ii. 285 *sq*.; Macaulay translates into Greek a dialogue in the *Rudens*, ii. 287.
PLINY the Elder, i. 466; ii. 418.
PLINY the Younger, i. 458; ii. 269, 387.
PLUNKET, Lord, Macaulay meets him at dinner, i. 242 *sq*.; Macaulay's eloquence likened to that of, i. 177.
PLUTARCH, Macaulay's estimate of, i. 448; *alluded to*, i. 42, 452, 468; ii. 285.
Plymouth Brethren, alluded to in rhyming doggrel, ii. 209.
Poets, "the only true," ii. 207; Professor Wilson's estimate of The Young Poets, ii. 123.
POLIGNAC, Prince, French Minister of Foreign Affairs under Charles X., i. 165 *sq*., 170, 173.
POLITIAN, ii. 417.
POLLOCK, Frederick (Lord Chief Baron), Brougham's rivalry with, on circuit, i. 148 *sq*.; ii. 324; at Macaulay's gathering of ex-Fellows of Trinity, ii. 410n.; *alluded to*, i. 218.

POLTIMORE, 1st Lord, i. 264.
Poor Richard's Almanac (by Benjamin Franklin), quoted, i. 338.
POPE, Alexander, his translation of a word in Homer, i. 228; certain touches in his poems suggested by Silius Italicus, i. 476; his pasquinade on Curll, a favourite of Macaulay's, ii. 372n.; his rough copy of the translation of the *Iliad* in the British Museum, ii. 400; Macaulay's youth nourished upon, ii. 455; alluded to, i. 221, 231, 418; ii. 110, 137n., 408; quoted, i. 182; ii. 42.
Popes:—Benedict XIV., ii. 30; Gregory XVI., ii. 31 sq.; Pius IX., ii. 200n.; Macaulay's favourite of the, ii. 30; his acquaintance with the list of, ii. 206.
PORSON, Richard, his criticism of Gibbon's attack on Christianity, ii. 40 and note; his Letters to Travis, ii. 40n., 293 and note; alluded to, ii. 437.
Portugal, affairs of, in 1833, i. 268, 303, 304 and note.
PRAED, W. M., at college with Macaulay, i. 78; his début in the House of Commons, i. 179, 209; alluded to, i. 83, 239, 450; quoted, i. 83n., 117; ii. 61.
Prayer-book, The English, purity of its language, ii. 24, 336; quoted, ii. 24, 336, 486.
Presbyterian administration of the Eucharist, ii. 336.
PRESCOTT, W. H., historian, his interest in the manuscript of Macaulay's *History*, ii. `229n.; Macaulay's remark on his *Philip the Second*, ii. 392.
Preston Races and the Earls of Derby, ii. 185.
PRESTON, Rev. M. M., of Shelford and Aspenden, i. 39–43, 470.
PRICE, ——, M.P. in 1831, i. 209.
PRIESTLEY, Dr., his house burned by a Birmingham mob in 1791, i. 162.
Prime Ministers in the 18th century, an accurate list of known but to few, ii. 105.
PRIOR, Matthew, Macaulay's perfect acquaintance with his poetry, ii. 455.
PROCOPIUS, Macaulay's mention of, in his *History* criticised, ii. 243.
Propertius, i. 452.
Prussia, King Frederick William III. of, likened to Attila, ii. 32.
Prussian Order of Merit, ii. 399 and note.
PULCI, Luigi, his *Morgante Maggiore*, ii. 393.
PUSEYITISM, Macaulay's dislike of, ii. 182, 200n., 201n., 290 sq.; his mention of High-Churchmen in his *History*, ii. 398n.; alluded to, ii. 208, 256, 258.
PYM, John, English patriot in Charles I.'s reign, i. 183.

Quakers, Macaulay's mention of, in his letters to his sisters, i. 263 *sq.*, 268, 307; ii. 209; the Cropper family, i. 292; he receives a deputation of, on the subject of William Penn, ii. 253 and note, 256; he has no love for their phraseology, ii. 291.

Quarterly Review, The, Croker's article on Macaulay's *History* in, ii. 242, 257; Macaulay's estimate of its political articles of 1830–1832, ii. 467 *sq.*; *alluded to*, i. 61, 390.

QUINTILIAN, i. 466.

QUINTUS CALABER (Smyrnæus), i. 452, 454.

QUINTUS CURTIUS, i. 465, 468.

Quotation, Macaulay feels the habit growing on him, i. 442; an unlucky, ii. 201; certain of Macaulay's favourite, ii. 243, 359; the quoting Doctor, i. 443*n.*; Macaulay's horror of misquotation, i. 55.

RACINE, i. 185, 476.

RADCLIFFE, Mrs., her *Mysteries of Udolpho*, i. 186.

Radicalism in Scotland in 1847, ii. 183.

RADNOR, 3rd Earl of, i. 264.

RALEIGH, Sir Walter, ii. 193; Cecil's compliment to, ii. 231.

RALPH, James, historian, ii. 322.

RAMOHUN ROY, i. 222; described by Sydney Smith, i. 224.

RANDOLPH, Dr. Thomas, Margaret Professor of Divinity at Oxford, one of Gibbon's assailants, ii. 289.

RANKE, Leopold von, his *History of the Papacy*, ii. 39; Knight of the Prussian Order of Merit, ii. 399*n.*; *quoted* for remark on Macaulay's writings, ii. 398.

RAPHAEL, his works, ii. 22, 42, 269.

RAVAILLAC, assassin of Henry IV. of France, ii. 445.

REEVE, Lovell, editor of *Literary Gazette*, offers to defend Macaulay about Penn, ii. 232.

Reform, Parliamentary, a dangerous topic in Pitt's time, i. 70; in 1830, i. 165, 172 *sq.*; in 1832, i. 257; "the pacific triumph of a great people," i. 291; Macaulay's wish to form a few commercial constituencies, i. 213; Revolution the only alternative of, in 1831, i. 252. See *Parliament*.

Reformers, their watchword in 1830–32, i. 287; the first great reformer, i. 443 *sq.*

Régime, the old, Macaulay's remark about, ii. 279.

REID, Thomas, metaphysician, ii. 248.

Rejected Addresses, ii. 455.

Religious "Confessions," ii. 302.

INDEX TO TREVELYAN'S LIFE OF MACAULAY. 73

Religious Worship, remark on attendance at, i. 289.
Repealers, The, a novel, i. 311.
REYNOLDS, Sir Joshua, his portrait of Fox, i. 219; of Garrick, i. 265; alluded to, ii. 210.
Rib, the river in Herts, i. 58.
RICE, Right Hon. Thomas Spring (1st Lord Monteagle), begs Macaulay to become Judge-Advocate in 1838, ii. 27 *sq.*; *alluded to,* i. 229, 242, 306, 359; ii. 7.
RICH, Henry, author of *What will the Lords do?* i. 296.
RICHARDSON, Samuel, novelist, i. 361; his *Clarissa Harlowe,* i. 249; ii. 138*n.*, 281; Macaulay's copy of it at Ootacamund, i. 385 and note; *Sir C. Grandison,* i. 61, 135, 210, 216, 266, 386*n.*, 471; ii. 138*n.*, 418; Macaulay could have probably re-written it from memory, i. 136.
RICHMOND, Duchess of, wife of 5th Duke, i. 236.
RICHMOND, 5th Duke of, i. 236; ii. 165.
RICHMOND, George, R.A., his portrait of Macaulay, ii. 278, 279*n.*
RIDLEY, Bishop, Macaulay's opinion of, ii. 475.
RIPON, 1st Earl of (Viscount Goderich), i. 306. See *Goderich.*
ROBERTS, David, R.A., ii. 41, 308, 430.
ROBERTSON, William, historian, i. 418; Macaulay not satisfied with his conception of history, ii. 274.
ROBINSON, H. Crabb, *quoted* for description of Macaulay in 1826, i. 125 *sq.*
ROEBUCK, J. A., M.P., i. 450; asks Macaulay to stand for the West Riding in 1848, ii. 248; consults him about standing for Liskeard, ii. 249; mutual goodwill between them, ii. 249, 258; his motion about the British Army in the Crimea, ii. 390*n.*
ROGERS, Samuel; the "oracle" of Holland House, i. 212; his seat there, i. 219; his esteem for Macaulay, i. 182, 212, 230, 243; his account of Scott and Byron, i. 222; his estimate of Byron's character, i. 223; Chantrey and the table, i. 231; his story of a certain couple, i. 267; in company with S. Smith, i. 222; entertains Macaulay at his house, i. 231 *sq.*, 346 *sq.*; ii. 198; is complimented by Macaulay in the *Edinburgh Review,* i. 221 and note; Macaulay's estimate of his poetry, i. 221, 342; of his prose, ii. 86; of his conversation, i. 225; a characteristic of him, i. 274; *alluded to,* i. 215, 296, 359.
ROLLIAD, The, i. 33; ii. 277.
Rome, Niebuhr's conjecture about burning men alive at, i. 446; Macaulay's visit to, ii. 29-42; Colosseum, ii. 269; English College at, ii. 31; St. Peter's, ii. 29 *sq.*, 37, 41 *sq.*, 49, 298, 416;

Rome (*continued*):—
three famous writers banished from, i. 478; Nero and the battle of the Metaurus, i. 479; the peculiarity of the oratory of the Roman tribunals, ii. 466; an old Roman inprecation, ii. 427.

Romilly, Sir John (Lord Romilly), at college with Macaulay, i. 78, 99, 226.

Romilly, Sir Samuel, Macaulay's reflections on his death, i. 92; his objection to reviewing his *Life*, ii. 116; his estimate of, ii. 276; *alluded to*, i. 248; ii. 100*n*.

Romney, G., painter, his *Life*, ii. 233.

Rookwood, a novel, by Ainsworth, ii. 46.

Rothley Temple, Leicestershire, Macaulay's birthplace, i. 25; described, i. 184 *sq.*; *alluded to*, i. 212, 280; ii. 435.

Roubiliac's cast of Pope at Rogers's house, i. 231.

Rousseau, Jean Jacques, his morbid sensibility, ii. 100*n.*; Macaulay's feeling towards him, ii. 278; *alluded to*, i. 362; ii. 286*n*.

Royal Academy. See *Academy, Royal*.

Rubens, Peter Paul, a picture of his at Leigh Court, ii. 330.

Rubini, Signor, i. 211.

Rupert, Prince, i. 283.

Ruskin, John, his comment on one of Titian's pictures, ii. 41; *alluded to*, ii. 417. 471.

Russell, Admiral (Earl of Orford), of La Hogue celebrity, ii. 439.

Russell, Lord (executed in 1683), his parting with his wife referred to by Macaulay, ii. 362 and note.

Russell, Lord, nephew of Lord J. Russell, i. 213 *sq.*, 218, 264.

Russell, Lord John (Earl Russell), introduces the Reform Bill in March, 1831, i. 175, 230; leads the attack upon the Tory Government in 1834, ii. 55; his notice of motion on the Corn Laws in 1841, ii. 89 *sq.*; attempts to form a Ministry in Dec., 1845, ii. 164-174; forms a Ministry in June, 1846, ii. 177; his Durham letter, ii. 200*n.*; presents Macaulay's brother with the living of Aldingham, ii. 264; his speech at Academy dinner in 1852, ii. 308; is defeated on Militia Bill in Feb., 1852, ii. 312; the Queen writes to him begging him to join the Aberdeen Ministry in Dec., 1852, ii. 339; Macaulay adds his persuasions on the same subject, ii. 340; his Reform Bill of 1854, ii. 375; his party defeated on the question of the China War in 1857, ii. 440; his resignation in June, 1866, ii. 64; his praise of Macaulay's oratory, i. 300, 317; Macaulay's regard for him, ii. 316; *alluded to*, i. 232 *sq.*, 237 *sq.*, 245*n.*, 248, 260, 264; ii. 51, 196, 296, 489.

Russia, its advance in civilization brought about by the languages of Western Europe, i. 411; Alexander I., Emperor of, i. 91; Nicholas, Emperor of, ii. 82.

Russian:—loan in 1832, i. 269; spy, i. 210; war of 1854, ii. 376-379.

RUTHERFORD, Lord (Right Hon. Andrew), Lord Brougham's attack on, in a pamphlet in 1856, ii. 441n.

RYAN, Sir Edward, Chief Justice in Calcutta, i. 431, 447, 472; ii. 219; his work as Chief Civil Service Commissioner, ii. 383n.

SADLER, Michael Thomas, M.P., his theory about population reviewed by Macaulay, i. 128 and note, 129; contests Leeds in 1832, i. 258, 294 sq.

ST. AULAIRE, M. de, French statesman in 1831, i. 237 sq.

St. James's parish, a deputation from, calls on Macaulay on the subject of the No-Popery agitation in 1850, ii. 200n.

St. Martin's summer, a, ii. 337.

ST. REAL, the Abbé de, his *Conjuration de Venise*, i. 390.

ST. SIMON, Duc de, his *Mémoires*, i. 134, 430; ii. 49, 274, 307.

St. Simonianism, doctrine founded by the Comte de St. Simon, ii. 467.

ST. VINCENT, 2nd Viscount, i. 242.

SAINTE-BEUVE, Charles Augustin de, *alluded to*, ii. 361.

Saints' Days, Macaulay's dislike to, ii. 76.

SALISBURY, 2nd Marquis of, ii. 306.

SALLUST, i. 448, 452; Macaulay's estimate of as an historian, i. 476.

SALVATOR ROSA, Macaulay pleased by a certain picture of, ii. 430.

SANCROFT, W., Archbishop of Canterbury, ii. 206.

SANDON, Lord (2nd Earl of Harrowby), his amendment to the Budget of 1841, ii. 89.

Saturnian metre, ii. 119; the only example of in English poetry, ii. 119.

SCARLETT, Sir James (1st Lord Abinger), his style of oratory, ii. 395, 466; not successful in the House of Commons, i. 179.

SCHILLER, J. C. F. von, how Macaulay ranked his Plays, ii. 209; his *Don Carlos*, ii. 233; violation of history in the last act of *Joan of Arc*, ii. 298 sq.; his *History of the War in the Netherlands*, ii. 459; *alluded to*, i. 263, 461, 473; ii. 210.

SCHLEGEL, Friedrich von, his estimate of the *Electra* of Euripides, i. 482.

SCHOLEFIELD, J., Greek Professor at Cambridge, ii. 437.

SCHOMBERG, Duke of, his grave in St. Patrick's Cathedral, Dublin, ii. 269 and note.

Scotch:—Church, ii. 93 and note, 182; entails, ii. 279*n*.; doctor in India, i. 385; peasantry, i. 44; people, ii. 453; relationship, i. 338; Revolution in 1688, ii. 106; sayings, i. 347, 372; Toryism, the old school of, ii. 319.

Scotchmen and High-Churchmen, ii. 398*n*.

Scotland; small number of electors in, in 1820, i. 160; agitation in, in 1840, ii. 81 *sq*.; Radicalism strong in, in 1847, ii. 183; Macaulay in, i. 67 and note, 335; ii. 223, 261 *sq*., 282, 336*n*., 481 *sq*.; declines to go there in Nov. 1857, ii. 439*n*. See *Edinburgh*.

SCOTT, Rev. Thomas, his religious "confessions," ii. 302.

SCOTT, Sir Walter, curiosity of some London servant-maids to see, i. 223; his last return to Scotland, i. 265; his death, i. 282; Macaulay objects to review Lockhart's *Life* of, ii. 8 *sq*.; Macaulay's estimate of his character, ii. 9; his love of ballads alluded to by Christopher North, ii. 123; his losses alluded to by H. Martineau, ii. 134; his name according to Miss Edgeworth not mentioned in Macaulay's first two volumes of the *History*, ii. 238; the boatman who had rowed him on the Lakes of Killarney, ii. 270; Mrs. Keith's advice to, about reading Afra Behn, ii. 465*n*.; his *Novels:*—ii. 138*n*.; Macaulay's eagerness to read while at Cambridge, i. 100*n*.; Macaulay remembers the publication of all of them, ii. 252; his fondness for making his characters repeat themselves, ii. 27; *Antiquary*, ii. 32; *Guy Mannering*, i. 373; *Montrose*, ii. 465; *Old Mortality*, ii. 465; *Surgeon's Daughter*, i. 307; *Waverley*, ii. 250, 465; his *Poetry :*—Macaulay finds a resemblance in Virgil to, i. 379; *Lady of the Lake*, ii. 472; *Lay*, Macaulay knew it by heart when seven years old, i. 31, 52; number of copies sold in the first year, ii. 250; characters in, ii. 472; *Marmion*, Macaulay's early delight in, i. 31; number of copies sold in the first month, ii. 250; *Rokeby*, Macaulay's estimate of, ii. 472; *Waterloo*, Macaulay buys it at Cambridge in 1815, ii. 439; *quoted*, ii. 36*n*.; *alluded to*, i. 58, 61, 94, 189, 222; ii. 319, 425.

SCOTT, Sir William (Lord Stowell), Peel's story of his timidity about speaking in Parliament, ii. 282*n*.

Scottish Reformation Society, Macaulay's reply to the, on the subject of the Edinburgh election of 1852, ii. 316.

SCRIBE, M., French comedy writer, i. 430.

Scutari column, Macaulay's inscription for the, ii. 379*n*., 380*n*.

SEAFORD, 1st Lord, i. 242.

SEDGWICK, Rev. A., Professor of Geology at Cambridge, i. 183; ii. 129.

Self-Tormentor, The, a novel, ii. 368.

SENECA, Lucius Annæus, Macaulay's dislike of his affectation, i. 456 sq., 469.
SENECA, M. Annæus, his *Controversiæ*, i. 456.
SENIOR, Nassau (Master in Chancery), ii. 105, 152, 339.
Sermon on the word "Therefore," ii. 323.
Servants, Mr. Littleton's, their refusal to live in Grosvenor Place, i. 242.
SETTLE, Elkanah, playwright, ii. 137n.
SEWARD, Anna, one of the bad writers Macaulay took pleasure in, i. 135, 153; ii. 477.
SHAFTESBURY, 1st Earl of, i. 471; ii. 367.
SHAFTESBURY, 3rd Earl of, ii. 367.
SHAFTESBURY, 7th Earl of, ii. 442.
SHAKESPEARE, William, Macaulay's estimate of, i. 380; ii. 202, 307; particular plays and characters:—*Antony*, ii. 19n.; *Hamlet*, ii. 203; *Henry V.*, i. 2; *Julius Cæsar*, ii. 279n.; *King John*, ii. 109, 306 and note; *Lear*, ii. 136n., 138n., 203, 233 sq.; *Macbeth*, i. 423; ii. 136n., 138n., 203; *Measure for Measure*, i. 2; *Merchant of Venice*, i. 417; ii. 458; *Much Ado*, ii. 365; *Othello*, i. 386; ii. 136n., 138n., 203, 232 sq.; *Pericles*, ii. 136n.; *Romeo*, ii. 233, 417; quotations from :—*All's well*, ii. 405; *Antony*, ii. 19n.; *Coriolanus*, i. 433; *Hamlet*, i. 310; ii. 247, 284; *Julius Cæsar*, ii. 47; *King John*, ii. 284, 306n.; *Macbeth*, i. 24n.; *Much Ado*, ii. 365; *Othello*, ii. 8; *Richard III.*, i. 324; ii. 284; *Romeo*, ii. 306n.; *Tempest*, i. 377; alluded to, i. 61, 418, 457; ii. 45, 268.
SHARP, Richard, known as "Conversation," his kindness to Macaulay as a young man, i. 182; his estimate of Lord Byron's character, i. 223; never talks scandal, i. 336; his sorrow on learning of Macaulay's Indian appointment, i. 344; his kindness to Hannah Macaulay, i. 359; Macaulay in a letter to him alludes to the habit of quotation, i. 442 sq.; his death, i. 344n.; *alluded to*, i. 211, 296, 358 sq., 361, 363; ii. 268.
SHARPE, Granville, on the Board of the Sierra Leone Company, i. 11.
SHAW, ——, of the firm of Spottiswoodes and Shaw, ii. 249.
SHAW, Frederic, M.P. in 1832, Recorder of Dublin, his obstruction in the House of Commons to the Orange Procession Bill, i. 275-277.
SHEIL, Mrs. i. 226.
SHEIL, R. L., M.P., his successful speech in the Reform Debate, March, 1831, i. 209; his dispute with Lord Althorp in the House of Commons in 1834, i. 365-367; remark of the *Times* on his being made a Privy Councillor, ii. 70; his death, i. 366n.; *alluded to*, i. 226, 297.

SHELBURNE, Earl of (4th Marquis of Lansdowne), M.P. for Calne, ii. 253, 256.
SHELLEY, Percy Bysshe, *quoted*, i. 327.
SHELLEY, Sir J., ii. 319.
SHENSTONE, William, ii. 408.
SHERIDAN, R. B., i. 161, 213; *quoted*, i. 117.
SHREWSBURY, Lady (wife of 11th Earl), referred to in an article on Duelling in the *Edinburgh Review*, ii. 115.
SHREWSBURY, 16th Earl of, ii. 32.
SIDTHORPE, Colonel, M.P. for Lincoln, i. 259, 273n., 276.
Sicilian Vespers, The, alluded to in the Notes on the Indian Penal Code, i. 424.
SIDDONS, Mrs., ii. 203.
SIDMOUTH, Lord. See *Addington*.
Sierra Leone, Company, i. 11–26, 37; religious factions at, i. 23.
Silius Italicus, i. 452, 476.
SIMEON, Rev. Charles, i. 39; ii. 20; great extent of his influence, i. 70n.
Simonides, i. 441.
SIMPSON, Sir James, ii. 316.
SINCLAIR, Sir John (writer on agriculture and statistics), his letter to Pitt about the Presidency of a Society, ii. 201; two "distinctions" in his works, ii. 201.
Sintram, a novel, ii. 209 *sq*.
SISMONDI, J. C. L. de, corresponded with Z. Macaulay, i. 66; his *Histoire des Français*, i. 361, 379; his *History of the Italian Republics*, ii. 21; Macaulay's interest in Pisa derived from the Pisan descent of, ii. 21.
SKELTON, John (Poet Laureate), ii. 412.
SKELTON, Philip, his *Deism Revealed*, ii. 391.
Slavery. See *Anti-Slavery question*.
SMITH, PAYNE & SMITH, Messrs., Bankers, ii. 420.
SMITH, Adam, his *Wealth of Nations*, ii. 138n.
SMITH, Albert, his allusion to Macaulay's election for Edinburgh in 1852, ii. 320.
SMITH, "Bobus," i. 347; talks to Macaulay about India, i. 358.
SMITH, Captain, at Arcot in 1834, i. 373; ii. 271.
SMITH, Sir Culling Eardley, contests the seat at Edinburgh in 1846, ii. 178, 188.
SMITH, Rev. J., the Demerara Missionary, i. 115 *sq*.
SMITH, John, school-fellow of Macaulay's, i. 60.
SMITH, John B., M.P. for Stockport in 1853, ii. 357.

SMITH, Rev. Sydney, Macaulay meets him at York, and goes to stay at Foston with him, i. 146 *sq.*; talks to him about Brougham, i. 193; in company with Rogers, i. 222; some *Boswelliana* of him, i. 224; makes sport of Lady Holland, i. 347; his *bon mot* about Royal Commissions, ii. 60; compared as a writer with Jeffrey, ii. 153; humorously described by Macaulay, ii. 197*n.*; his *Edinburgh Review* articles, ii. 272; his qualities, mental and moral, compared with Jeffrey's, ii. 278; his remark on Macaulay's "flashes of silence," ii. 332*n.*; *quoted,* i. 73; ii. 332*n.*; *alluded to,* i. 210, 358 *sq.*

SMITH, Vernon (Lord Lyveden), i. 240, 303; ii. 68, 415*n.*; his motion about Lord Ellenborough in 1843, ii. 140.

SMITH, Mrs. Vernon, i. 240.

SMITH, William, Unitarian M.P., one of the "Clapham Sect," i. 63,

SMITH, Dr. William, *quoted* for meaning of the word "xystus," ii. 408*n.*

71.

SMITHERS ———, name of a criminal mentioned in one of Macaulay's doggrel verses, i. 268.

SMOLLETT, Tobias, novelist and historian, i. 336; ii. 218; Macaulay's estimate of his *History of England,* ii. 36, 322; Charles Lamb *quoted* for remark on, ii. 36*n.*; *quoted,* i. 222.

SMYTHE, Hon. G., M.P. for Canterbury 1841–1847 (7th Viscount Strangford), one of the "Young England" party, ii. 133.

SOANE, Sir John, architect, ii. 416.

Socialists, their fears about the Great Exhibition of 1851, ii. 297.

SOCRATES, Macaulay not impressed with his character, i. 445; ii. 369, 371.

SOMERS, Lord (Lord Chancellor), ii. 441; his love of ancient literature, ii. 431.

SOMERSET, Duke of, Protector, ii. 439.

SOMERVILLE, Thomas, a bad writer of history, ii. 322.

SOMERVILLE, 15th Lord, President of the Scotch Agricultural Society, ii. 201.

SOPHOCLES, fortunate for his fame that so few of his plays are extant, ii. 456; Macaulay's estimate of his plays, i. 481; how ranked by him among the poets, ii. 202; *quoted,* i. 444, 481; *alluded to,* i. 91, 444, 450, 452; ii. 22, 109, 304.

SOTHEBY, William, i. 153; his translation of the *Iliad,* i. 228 *sq.*

SOUTHEY, Robert, Macaulay's review of his *Colloquies* referred to by Professor Wilson, i. 142; ranked below Rogers as a poet by Byron and others, i. 221; his broken state of health in 1841, ii.

SOUTHEY, Robert (*continued*):—
85; the invention of historical essays due to him, ii. 109; his power of writing simultaneously on many subjects, ii. 128; his own estimate of his writings, ii. 135; Macaulay's opinion of his *Common-place Book*, ii. 264; his worth depicted in Coleridge's correspondence, ii. 426 and note; Macaulay's estimate of his writings and character, ii. 468 *sq.*; *alluded to*, i. 59 *sq.*, 390, 418.

Spain, King of, Ferdinand VII., his death, i. 282.

Spanish ballads, Lockhart's versions of, better than the originals, ii. 278.

Spanish comedies translated, a "bright speck" in the Macaulays' library at Clapham, ii. 297.

Spanish Stock, Macaulay's definition of the different classes of, ii. 420.

Spectator, The, i. 57; ii. 455; "Sir Roger de Coverley," i. 296; "Honeycomb," ii. 285; Byrom's lines to Joanna Bentley in, ii. 366*n*.

SPENCER, 3rd Earl. See *Althorp, Lord*.

SPENCER, 4th Earl, i. 246; ii. 274 *sq.*

SPENSER, Edmund, his *Faëry Queen*, ii. 125, 138*n*.

Sponge's Sporting Tour, a novel, ii. 472.

SPOTTISWOODES, Messrs., Printers, i. 172; a tribute to Macaulay's clearness of style from their office, ii. 235.

SPURZHEIM, J. G., a votary of, who had prophesied Macaulay's success, ii. 311*n*.

STAËL, Madame de, corresponded with Z. Macaulay, i. 66; "the first woman of her age," i. 246; Macaulay's estimate of her *De l'Allemagne*, i. 246.

STAINFORTH, George, school-fellow of Macaulay's, i. 40.

STANFIELD, Clarkson, R.A., ii. 308, 430.

STANHOPE, Earl. See *Mahon, Lord*.

STANHOPE, Miss (Lady Mary), afterwards Countess Beauchamp, Macaulay's Valentine to, ii. 213, 297, 413.

STANLEY, A. P., Dean of Westminster, ii. 3*n*.

STANLEY, Edward (14th Earl of Derby), mention of his eloquence, i. 178, 198, 247 *sq.*, 297, 450; his avowal of timidity on rising to speak, i. 247; Macaulay's remark on his oratory, i. 247; ii. 441; and description of him as "a clever boy," ii. 253; compliments Macaulay on a speech, i. 234; his Resolution on Slavery Bill, i. 312, 316, 320; Prime Minister in 1852, ii. 312; Lord Maidstone's prediction concerning, ii. 330; speech at Academy Dinner in 1852, ii. 308; at Oxford Commemoration, ii. 399*n*.; *alluded to*, i. 246, 275; ii. 140, 431.

STANLEY, Lord (15th Earl of Derby), ii. 351, 399n.
STANLEY OF ALDERLEY, 2nd Lord, ii. 61 and note.
STATIUS, i. 452, 470, 476; *quoted*, i. 466.
STAUNTON, Sir G., ii. 201.
STEELE, Richard, ii. 116, 455.
STEELE, Tom, an O'Connellite, ii. 6.
STEPHEN, Fitzjames (Mr. Justice), his estimate of the Indian Penal Code, i. 425–427.
STEPHEN, James, brother-in-law of W. Wilberforce, i. 70n., 282, 327.
STEPHEN, Sir James, i. 64; his article on the Clapham Sect in the *Edinburgh Review*, i. 69n., 70n.; Crabb Robinson meets Macaulay in 1825 at his house, i. 126; his letter to Fanny Macaulay on her father's death, ii. 2; Modern History Professor at Cambridge, ii. 265 and note; writes to Macaulay on the publication of the 3rd and 4th vols. of his *History*, ii. 394; *quoted*, i. 14n., 65.
STEPHENS, Catherine (afterwards Countess of Essex), Macaulay hears her sing at Cambridge in 1820, ii. 439.
STERNE, Laurence, his *Tristram Shandy* alluded to, i. 31n., 462; ii. 218.
STEWART, Dugald, i. 460; ii. 124, 248, 381; Macaulay dislikes his mode of writing biography, ii. 292.
STIRLING, Fanny, actress, her acting in *Masks and Faces*, ii. 214.
STIRLING-MAXWELL, Sir William, his account of Macaulay and Jeffrey, with reference to *Paradise Lost*, i. 53n.; of Macaulay's remembrance of some doggrel verse, i. 54n.; on first meeting Macaulay, mistakes him for a General, i. 122n.
STOCKDALE, Percival, miscellaneous writer, 1736–1811; Macaulay's estimate of his powers not high, ii. 426.
STODDART, ——, Macaulay in 1822 tutor to his sons, i. 110.
STOPFORD, Admiral Sir R. (Commander-in-Chief of the British Squadron at the capture of Acre in 1840), ii. 111.
STOTHARD, Thomas, R.A., his *Byron* illustrations at Holland House, i. 219; a book-case painted by him at Rogers's, i. 231.
STOWE, Mrs. Beecher, ii. 366; what Macaulay proposes to give her, ii. 367; her *Sunny Memories* full of blunders, ii. 367; her account of Macaulay's remarks on cathedrals, ii. 367; an instance of a discarded favourite, ii. 252n.
Stradivarius, George Eliot's poem, *quoted*, ii. 230 *sq.*
STRAFFORD, Earl of (Sir John Byng), Macaulay refers a duelling challenge to, ii. 6 *sq.*
STRAFFORD, Earl of (Wentworth), a parallel drawn in Calcutta between Macaulay and, i. 455.
STRANGE, Sir Robert, engraver, his *Letter to Lord Bute* (1775), ii. 395.

STRAWBERRY Hill, Macaulay's visit to, when a child, i. 28.
STRUTT, Edward, M.P. (Lord Belper), college contemporary of Macaulay's, i. 78, 226, 249; ii. 318.
STRUTT, Mrs., ii. 202.
STRUTTS, The, ii. 202.
STRYPE, John, his *Lives* of the founders of the Anglican Church, ii. 474.
SUE, Eugene, his novels, ii. 371, 388.
SUETONIUS, i. 457; ii. 322.
SUGDEN, Edward, M.P. (Lord St. Leonards), i. 114; ii. 61, 77.
SULIVAN, L., Assistant Secretary at War in 1840, his assurance of Macaulay's accuracy in an Army Estimate, ii. 73.
SUNDERLAND, Earl of, James II.'s Prime Minister, ii. 91.
SUTHERLAND, J. C., *alluded to* by Macaulay in his Indian Minutes, i. 413, 416.
SUTTON, Charles Manners, Archbishop of Canterbury, i. 138.
SWIFT, Jonathan, Dean of St. Patrick's, his habit of observing his birthday as a day of sorrow, ii. 18 and note; his inscription on Schomberg's tablet in St. Patrick's, ii. 269 and note; his bust, ii. 270; *allusions* to him or his *Writings*, i. 138, 418; ii. 9, 110, 267, 392, 455; *quoted*, ii. 353, 365.

Table-turning in Macaulay's chambers, ii. 311.
TACITUS, one of the few historians admired by Macaulay, ii. 274; compared with Thucydides, i. 457 *sq.*; *alluded to*, i. 97, 476; ii. 109, 437.
TAGLIONI, Mdlle., dancer, i. 273*n*.
TALFOURD, Serjeant (Sir T. Noon), his Copyright Bill, ii. 135 *sq.*; Macaulay's estimate of his *Ion*, i. 459.
TALLEYRAND, Prince, Macaulay meets him at Holland House, i. 237; description of his personal appearance, i. 237; his talent for anecdotes, i. 238.
TASSO, Torquato, i. 379; ii. 109; not a favourite of Macaulay's, ii. 35.
TAUCHNITZ, Baron, sale of his edition of 3rd and 4th vols. of Macaulay's *History*, ii. 398.
TAVISTOCK, Marquis of (afterwards 7th Duke of Bedford), i. 213, 241.
TAYLOR, Sir Henry, Macaulay's opinion of his *Van Artevelde*, i. 459.
TEIGNMOUTH, Lord, Governor-General of India, i. 70*n*.; his house at Clapham the cradle of the Bible Society, i. 73.
TENNYSON, Alfred, Poet Laureate, ii. 284; Macaulay's admiration of his *Guinevere*, ii. 481; his *In Memoriam* quoted, ii. 292*n*.
TENTERDEN, Lord, Chief Justice of England, his early proficiency in Greek and Latin versification, ii. 381.

TERENCE, i. 452 *sq.*
TERRY, Miss Kate, actress, ii. 306 and note.
THACKERAY, William Makepeace, his own life to be traced in his novels, i. 2; his account of Macaulay being preferred as a sight to a hippopotamus, ii. 259; Macaulay goes to one of his *Lectures on the English Humourists* in 1851, ii. 299; *Lovel the Widower*, in the first number of the *Cornhill Magazine*, found by Macaulay's side at his death, ii. 488; Macaulay finds fault with his description of the religious element of Clapham in *The Newcomes*, i. 62-64; Macaulay at a college breakfast-party in 1858 compares himself to Major Pendennis, ii. 438; *Rebecca and Rowena*, ii. 275; quoted, for Macaulay's account to him of *Clarissa Harlowe* in India, i. 385; the "Windsor Castle" address, ii. 71; "Right Hon. T. B. Maconkey," ii. 71n.; on Macaulay's wonderful industry, ii. 220.
Thames, the river, a fine subject for a descriptive poem, ii. 388.
THEOCRITUS, i. 452, 466, 470; ii. 369n.
THEOPHRASTUS, i. 452; translation of some words of his at an examination in Calcutta, i. 453.
THESIGER, Sir F. (Lord Chancellor Chelmsford), ii. 307.
THIERS, Louis Adolphe, historian and statesman, his policy on the Eastern Question in 1840, ii. 82 *sq.*; his qualities as an historian discussed at a breakfast-party, ii. 199; Macaulay's remark to him about Palmerston, ii. 307; Macaulay's estimate of parts of the *Histoire du Consulat et de l'Empire*, ii. 273 *sq.*, 320.
THIRLWALL, Connop, Bishop of St. David's, entertains Macaulay and his sisters at Cambridge in 1831, i. 183; retires from his tutorship on account of a pamphlet of his, i. 437, 438 and note; his *History of Greece*, i. 470; Macaulay meets him and Whewell at Monckton Milnes's, ii. 437; "the Thirlwall of Calcutta," i. 453.
THOMPSON, Alderman, M.P. for the City of London in 1831, i. 207.
THOMSON, James, his *Edward and Eleonora*, i. 462.
THORNHILL, Richard, his duel with Dering referred to in the *Edinburgh Review*, ii. 116.
THORNTON, Henry, M.P. for Southwark, friend of W. Wilberforce, appointed Chairman of the Sierra Leone Company, i. 12; introduces a Bill in 1799 about the African slave-trade, i. 71; *alluded to*, i. 21, 73; ii. 3, 17.
THORNTON, Henry Sykes, son of preceding, at Cambridge with Macaulay, i. 75; Macaulay's banker, ii. 420; his classification of Spanish stock, ii. 420; thought Stephen's remarks on Z. Macaulay in the *Edinburgh Review* unfriendly, i. 70n.

THORNTON, John, the earliest of the Claphamites, i. 63.
THORPE, Rev. Dr., i. 132, 243, 268.
THRALE, Mrs., her *Anecdotes* of Dr. Johnson, i. 233.
THUCYDIDES, ranked by Macaulay as the first of all historians, i. 475; ii. 248; one of the three greatly admired by him, ii. 274; his 7th book the *ne plus ultra* of human art, i. 449; ii. 392; not appreciated by the young, i. 440; *alluded to*, i. 452, 455, 458; ii. 109, 241, 249, 470.
THURLOW, Lord Chancellor, his house in Great Ormond Street the home of the Macaulays, i. 130; Macaulay thinks Lord Campbell's estimate of him unfair, ii. 277; *alluded to*, ii. 67.
THURLOW, 2nd Lord (Edward Hovell), his poetry, ii. 198.
THURTELL, John, the murderer of Mr. Weare, i. 187.
TIBERIUS, the Emperor, i. 476.
TIBULLUS, i. 452.
TICKNOR, George, his *Spanish Literature* recommended by Macaulay to Queen Victoria, ii. 306.
TIECK, Ludwig, novelist and poet, i. 473; his complaint about his countrymen, ii. 472.
TIERNEY, Right Hon. George, M.P., on the authorship of *Junius*, i. 190; hears his own character as drawn by Francis, i. 195; confesses to nervousness when rising to speak in the House of Commons, i. 209, 247; a ready and fluent speaker, i. 247.
TILLOTSON, John, Archbishop of Canterbury, a favourite of Macaulay's, i. 438; ii. 475.
TILTEY, Rev. John, of Llanrwst, i. 105.
TINDAL, N. C., Lord Chief Justice of the Common Pleas, Macaulay meets at Sydney Smith's, i. 147.
TITIAN, ii. 41, 113.
TONE, Theobald Wolfe, projector of the society of United Irishmen in 1791, his *Memoirs*, ii. 267.
TONSON, Jacob, publisher, his treatment of Dryden, i. 351.
Toryism :—death-knell of its golden age, i. 162; broken up into factions in 1843, ii. 133; the old school of Scotch, ii. 319.
Tower Hamlets, Macaulay asked to address the electors of, in 1833, i. 345.
TOWNSHEND, Charles, Chancellor of the Exchequer in 1766, i. 342, 451.
TRAJAN, Pliny's *Panegyric* on, ii. 387.
TRAVIS, Archdeacon, Letters to. See *Porson*.
TREBELLIUS CAPITOLINUS, ii. 268.
TREVELYAN ———, Macaulay's niece who died as an infant, i. 434; ii. 27 and note.

TREVELYAN, Alice, Macaulay's letter to about his garden, ii. 408n.;
his dream about her and Pepys's *Diary*, ii. 428; *alluded to*, ii. 208,
259 *sq.*, 281, 390, 414n., 415, 481, 483.

TREVELYAN, George Otto, M.P., Macaulay's letter to him touching
Greek writers, ii. 432 *sq.*; Macaulay's lines on Palmerston added
to a Harrow prize poem of, ii. 434; his college breakfast-party
with Macaulay in the character of *Major Pendennis*, ii. 438;
alluded to, ii. 216 *sq.*, 390, 432, 434, 436, 461n.

TREVELYAN, H. W., Lieutenant (afterwards Major-General), i. 392.

TREVELYAN, Margaret (wife of 2nd Sir Henry Holland), Macaulay's
affection for, embodied in a passage in his *Virginia*, ii. 124;
extracts of letters of his to her, ii. 207; her marriage, ii. 479;
alluded to, i. 428, 450, 457, 460, 463, 465; ii. 53, 74, 207n.,
216 *sq.*, 236, 299, 323, 325, 345, 390, 395, 404, 414n., 427.

TREVELYAN, Sir Charles, Bart., K.C.B., his engagement to Hannah
Macaulay, i. 391; Macaulay's description of, i. 391-395, 435 *sq.*;
appointed Assistant-Secretary of the Treasury, ii. 72; abused in
the *Morning Post* in 1849, ii. 266; draws up a Report on Civil
Service Reform, ii. 383; appointed Governor of Madras in 1859,
ii. 479; *alluded to*, i. 135, 396, 414, 434, 442, 450, 457, 460; ii.
217, 232n., 234, 273, 380, 386, 436.

TREVELYAN, Sir John, of Nettlecombe, 5th Bart, i. 436.

TREVELYANS, The (Sir Charles's family), ii. 99, 202, 232, 413, 415,
417, 426.

TRIBONIAN, i. 454.

Trinity College, Dublin, a translation of some words of Theophrastus
by a graduate of, i. 453.

TROLLOPE, Mrs. Frances, her *Domestic Manners of the Americans*, ii.
117, 122.

TRYPHIODORUS, ii. 437.

TUFNELL, Right Hon. H., M.P., Treasury Whip in 1848, ii. 249 and
note.

Tunbridge Wells, Macaulay at, in 1853, ii. 357, 368-373; description
of in the 3rd chapter of the *History*, ii. 368n.

TURENNE, Marshal, i. 88.

TURTON, Bishop, his Vindication of Porson from the animadversions of
Bishop Burgess, ii. 293.

TUSCANY, Cosmo Grand Duke of, his *Travels*, ii. 263.

TWISS, Horace, M.P., in the House of Commons, 22 March, 1831,
i. 208.

TYLER, Wat, alluded to in the Notes on the Penal Code, i. 424.

Uncle Tom's Cabin, Macaulay's estimate of, ii. 329.
Unitarians, the Whig candidates for Leeds in 1832 reported to be, i. 289; remark about, with reference to religious worship and voting at elections, i. 289 *sq.*; in 1874 the most over-represented sect in Great Britain, i. 290.
University Calendars, Macaulay's intimate acquaintance with the Oxford and Cambridge, i. 85; ii. 352, 436, 459.
Useful Knowledge, Society for the Diffusion of, i. 459.
Utilitarians, the, Charles Austin at Cambridge imbued with the ideas of, i. 79; Macaulay's attack on, i. 140 *sq.*; their praise of Croker in the *Westminster Review*, i. 254.

VALERIUS MAXIMUS, i. 456.
VAN DE WEYER, M. (Belgian Envoy at the Court of St. James's), remarks on the English horror of false quantities, ii. 201; Macaulay meets Thiers at his house, ii. 307; *alluded to*, ii. 196, 198 *sq.*, 471*n*.
Van Diemen's Land, i. 380.
VANE, Lord Harry, ii. 199.
VAUGHAN, Dr. C. J., Head-master of Harrow School, ii. 432, 434.
VELLEIUS PATERCULUS, i. 452, 476.
Venice. See *Daru*, and *St. Real*.
VERNEY, ——, Macaulay meets at Naples, ii. 46.
VERNON, E. V., Archbishop of York, i. 138.
Versification, Greek and Latin. See *Macaulay—Remarks, etc.*
VICTORIA, Queen, coronation of, ii. 10; her kindness to Leigh Hunt, ii. 85; her visit to France in 1843, ii. 148; her popularity in Ireland, ii. 271*n.*; conversation with Macaulay about his *History*, ii. 279; amused by Macaulay's stories, ii. 295; her letter to Lord J. Russell, ii. 339 *sq.*; *alluded to*, ii. 311, 377, 435.
Village Belles, The, a novel, i. 322.
VILLEMAIN, Abel François, French statesman and author, ii. 465.
VILLIERS, Charles P., M.P. (Right Hon.), at Cambridge with Macaulay, i. 78 and note, 80; his annual motion against the Corn-Laws, ii. 188.
VILLIERS, Edward (brother of 4th Earl of Clarendon), i. 270.
VILLIERS, George. See *Clarendon*, 4th Earl of.
VILLIERS, Hyde (brother of 4th Earl of Clarendon), at Cambridge with Macaulay, i. 78 and note, 80; Macaulay's high opinion of, i. 270; his illness and death, i. 282, 292, 295; Macaulay succeeds him as Secretary to the Board of Control, i. 292.

VIRGIL, some lines of his the finest in the Latin language, i. 379; his description of Italian landscape, ii. 29; his tomb, ii. 44; how Macaulay ranked him among poets, ii. 202; *alluded to,* i. 228, 325, 443*n.*, 448, 470; ii. 22, 369*n.*

VIZETELLY, Henry, publisher of an unauthorised edition of Macaulay's *Speeches,* ii. 372-374.

VOLTAIRE (F. M. Arouet), Macaulay's inscription for a picture of, i. 145; Macaulay's project of writing an article on, i. 362; his estimate of some lines in Virgil, i. 379; his vein of ridicule inferior to Plato's, i. 445; Ninon de l'Enclos and, i. 471; a bust of, in Macaulay's chambers, ii. 100; Macaulay visits Ferney, ii. 100*n.*; Collins's account of, ii. 100*n.*; his "Diatribe of Dr. Akakia," ii. 372*n.*; *alluded to,* i. 197, 361, 418; ii. 107, 274, 296, 431; *quoted,* ii. 473.

VOPISCUS, ii. 268.

VYVYAN, Sir R., M.P., leader of a Tory faction in 1843, ii. 133.

WADDINGTON, H., Dean of Durham, ii. 410*n.*

WAITHMAN, R. (Alderman), M.P. for the City of London, 1826-1832, i. 97.

WALDEGRAVE, Countess, wife of the 4th Earl, Macaulay's visit to at Strawberry Hill when four years old, i. 28.

WALDEGRAVES, The, i. 347.

Wales, a Cambridge reading party in, i. 104-106.

WALKER, George, Bishop of Derry, ii. 225 and note, 282*n.*

WALKER, Mr., and his "yellow girls," i. 187.

WALKER, Sidney, at Cambridge with Macaulay, i. 78.

WALLACE, W., editor of Mackintosh's *History of England,* his quarrel with Macaulay, ii. 4-7.

WALPOLE, Horace (brother of Sir R. Walpole), diplomatist, how described by Smollett, ii. 37.

WALPOLE, Horace (4th Earl of Orford), i. 134, 335; ii. 109, 367. See *Macaulay—Writings.*

WALPOLE, Sir Robert, Prime Minister, i. 179, 239; ii. 55, 367.

WALTERS, W. C., on a college reading party with Macaulay, i. 105.

WARBURTON, W., Bishop of Gloucester, his *Divine Legation* likened by Macaulay to Buckle's *Civilisation,* ii. 470*n.*; his *Julian,* ii. 473; his Letters to Bishop Hurd, ii. 475.

WARDELL, J., his *History of Leeds,* ii. 221 and note.

WARE, Ebenezer, on a college reading party with Macaulay, i. 105.

Warming-Pan Story, The, *alluded to,* ii. 377.

WARREN, Samuel, his *Ten Thousand a Year,* ii. 468.

WATERLOO, Battle of, mentioned at a public meeting in Calcutta, i. 406; Macaulay's unsuccessful prize-poem on, i. 94 *sq.*; *alluded to*, ii. 340, 400.
WATSON, Dr. (Sir Thomas), ii. 486.
WATSON, R. (Bishop of Llandaff), Gibbon's critic, ii. 289*n*. 290.
WATSON, R., M.P. for Canterbury, i. 296.
WATTS, Dr. Isaac, *quoted*, i. 46.
WEARE, William, murdered by Thurtell in 1823, i. 187.
WEISSEMBOURG, M. de, Macaulay meets at Holland House, i. 240.
WELLESLEY, Marquis, Governor-General of India, i. 240; meets at the Duchess of Kent's, i. 309 *sq.*; his taste and liberality in India, i. 375; his reputation at school and college, ii. 352, 381.
WELLINGTON, Duke of, and the Catholic Relief Bill, i. 163*n.*; his advice about speaking in House of Commons, ii. 202; his oath, ii. 257 and note; his staff-officer, ii. 281 *sq.*; on the loss of the *Birkenhead*, ii. 308; his praise of Macaulay's *History*, ii. 253; Lawrence's portrait of, ii. 33; *alluded to*, i. 9, 143, 165, 172 *sq.*, 213, 250 *sq.*, 253, 259 *sq.*, 304*n.*, 329, 375, 377, 406; ii. 57, 111, 132, 140, 340, 379, 400.
WELSTED, Leonard, his *Life and Remains*, ii. 391.
WESLEY, John, ii. 302, 371; his *Life* by Southey, ii. 468.
WEST, Benjamin (President of the Royal Academy), ii. 269.
Westminster:—Abbey, Hall, School. See *London.*
WESTMINSTER, Archbishop of. See *Wiseman.*
WESTMINSTER, 2nd Marquis of, i. 332, 434*n.*
Westminster Review, and Macaulay's article on Croker, i. 254.
Weston House, i. 283.
WETHERELL, Sir Charles (Attorney-General in the Duke of Wellington's Administration), i. 114, 254.
What will the Lords do? a pamphlet by Rich, i. 296.
WHATELY, R., Archbishop of Dublin, his *Logic*, i. 470.
WHEWELL, Dr. W. (Master of Trinity College, Cambridge), Macaulay's letter to, about Praed, i. 179; entertains Macaulay and his sisters at Cambridge in 1831, i. 183 *sq.*; Macaulay not a favourite of his, i. 184; "a ruddy strapping divine" in 1820, ii. 31; discusses moral obligations with Hallam and Macaulay at a breakfast, ii. 199; at dinner at *The Club*, ii. 201; an "arch-sceptic" about clairvoyance, ii. 310; meets Thirlwall and Macaulay at Monckton Milnes's, ii. 437.
Whig Party, the:—in 1831, i. 181; in 1839, ii. 64; in 1841, ii. 88, 92; at Edinburgh in 1847, ii. 183; Brougham's abuse of, ii. 11, 139; as Free-traders, ii. 88.

WHITAKER, Rev. J. (Fellow of Corpus Christi College, Oxford), an assailant of Gibbon's, ii. 280.
WHITE, H. Kirke, ii. 469.
WHITFIELD, Rev. George, his religious "Confessions," ii. 302.
WILBERFORCE, Robert, son of William Wilberforce, ii. 310.
WILBERFORCE, Samuel, successively Bishop of Oxford, and of Winchester, dines at *The Club*, ii. 201; Lord Carlisle's notice of a breakfast at his house, ii. 203*n*.; thinks the mesmeriser's description of Macaulay as an "historical painter" very just, ii. 310; the clairvoyante at his house, ii. 310; loses his temper on the subject of clairvoyance at the Bishop of London's dinner, ii. 311; a pall-bearer at Macaulay's burial, ii. 489; *alluded to*, i. 64, 366*n*.; ii. 209.
WILBERFORCE, William, two entries in his Diary on the subject of the Slave-trade, i. 71; his Toryism, i. 96; his reference to Macaulay's speech at the Anti-Slavery meeting in 1824, i. 116; his testimony to Macaulay's good humour, i. 125; his remark to Hannah Macaulay about her father and brother, i. 144; his reminiscence of Parliamentary life, i. 144; story of Fox, Pitt, and him, i. 194 *sq.*; his death, i. 326; burial, i. 316, 329; his *Life*, ii. 387; *alluded to*, i. 11, 21, 64, 66, 70*n*., 72, 151 *sq.*, 270; ii. 3, 89, 201.
WILBERFORCE, William, eldest son of preceding, at Shelford school with Macaulay, i. 41.
WILKES, John, the lemon he squeezed for Johnson at Mr. Dilly's dinner, i. 187.
WILKIE, Sir David, i. 324.
WILKIE, W., D.D., his poem *The Epigoniad*, i. 379.
WILKINS, William, architect of the National Gallery, ii. 416.
WILKINSON, Moses, a Wesleyan Methodist preacher at Sierra Leone, i. 23.
WILKS, ——, Rev., "poor little Wilks," i. 268.
WILLIAM III., the Greaves Prize at Trinity College, Cambridge, for best essay on, i. 86–89; the ruling passion of his life, ii. 198; Wellington's cold language about the death of a staff-officer reminds Macaulay of, ii. 282.
WILLIAM IV., his offer of the Garter to Earl Grey in 1831, i. 212; coronation of, i. 236, 249–251; his action about the Reform Bill in May, 1832, i. 259 *sq.*, 306, 307 and note; about the Irish Church Bill in 1833, i. 308; calls Sir R. Peel to power in Nov. 1834, i. 443*n*.; ii. 55; likened by Macaulay to Jove in the *Prometheus*, i. 444*n*.
WILLIAMS & DEACON, Messrs., Macaulay's bankers, ii. 419 *sq*.

WILSON, Daniel, Minister of St. John's Chapel, Bedford Row, afterwards Bishop of Calcutta, i. 132, 224; receives Hannah Macaulay in his house at Calcutta, i. 370.

WILSON, Right Hon. James (Financial Member of the Council of India in 1859), i. 435.

WILSON, Professor John (Christopher North), his attacks on Macaulay in *Blackwood's Magazine*, i. 142; Macaulay objects to enter into a contest with him on the subject of Croker's *Boswell*, i. 255; praises the *Lays of Ancient Rome* in *Blackwood*, ii. 122-124; Macaulay affected by his generosity for so doing, ii. 126; votes for Macaulay at the Edinburgh election of 1852, ii. 319.

WINCKELMANN, J. J., writer on art, ii. 16.

Windermere, Macaulay's visit to in 1859, ii. 481.

Windsor Castle, a horse offered to Macaulay while staying at, i. 123 *sq.*; his visit to, in 1851, ii. 294-296; in 1852, when he sees *King John* played, ii. 306; occasional visits to, ii. 413; he dates an address to his constituents from, in 1839, ii. 70, 71 and note, 74-76; its name gives him a twinge twelve years later, ii. 294.

WISEMAN, Dr. (Cardinal Archbishop of Westminster), Macaulay visits at the English College in Rome, ii. 31 *sq.*; does not alarm Macaulay in 1850, ii. 291 *sq.*

WOLFE TONE. See *Tone*.

WOLMAR, a courier, ii. 364.

WOOD, Sir Charles, M.P. (afterwards Lord Halifax), in the House of Commons, March 22, 1831, i. 208; expresses to Macaulay his pleasure at the well-timed appearance of his *History*, ii. 237; his Indian Civil Service Bill in 1853, ii. 346-348, 351; appoints Macaulay Chairman of the Committee for arranging the system of open competition for Indian appointments, ii. 380.

WOODHOUSE, Robert, mathematician, i. 91.

WOODROW, H., Editor of a Collection of Macaulay's Indian Education Minutes, i. 413*n.*; extracts from the collection, i. 413-419; *quoted* touching the number of erasures in the Minutes, ii. 229*n.*

WOOLNER, Thomas, his statue of Macaulay at Cambridge, i. 123.

WORCESTER, Bishop of (R. J. Carr), i. 264.

Worcester Musical Festival in 1851, ii. 300.

WORDSWORTH, Christopher, Master of Trinity College, Cambridge, i. 438*n.*

WORDSWORTH, William, his merits as a poet discussed by Macaulay and his contemporaries at Cambridge, i. 80; not a favourite of Macaulay's, ii. 331; Byron's preference for Gifford and Rogers to, i. 342; Macaulay visits his tomb at Grasmere, ii. 481;

WORDSWORTH, William (*continued*):—
"Macaulay standing by the grave of," the most sublime of all spectacles, ii. 481; *alluded to*, ii. 408; his Writings:—the *Prelude*, ii. 135; Macaulay thinks it unreadable, i. 80 *sq.*; his criticism on it, ii. 283 *sq.*; the *Excursion*, ii. 283 *sq.*; *Sonnets* and *Ode to Immortality*, ii. 135; *quoted*, ii. 327 *sq.*
Wrington, Somersetshire, Macaulay visits in 1852, ii. 325, 328.
WYNNE, Right Hon. C. W. W., M.P., i. 317.

XENOPHON, i. 452, 458; ii. 433; Macaulay's admiration of the *Anabasis*, i. 475.
XENOPHON, the Ephesian, author of the *Ephesiaca*, Macaulay thinks his novel the basest thing in Greek, i. 465 and note, 466 and note.

York, its population in 1685, ii. 221.
YORK, Duchess of, her cemetery for sixty-four dogs at Oatlands, ii. 415*n*.
YORK, Duke of, i. 72.
YOUNG, Edward, author of *Night Thoughts*, quoted, ii. 208.
YOUNG, John, his *Lectures on Intellectual Philosophy*, i. 418.
"Young Poets, The," Christopher North's depreciation of, ii. 123.

www.ingramcontent.com/pod-product-compliance
Lightning Source LLC
Chambersburg PA
CBHW031119160426
43192CB00008B/1042